Jews and Christians

The Myth of a Common Tradition

JEWS AND CHRISTIANS

The Myth of a Common Tradition

JACOB NEUSNER

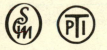

SCM PRESS
London

TRINITY PRESS INTERNATIONAL
Philadelphia

First Published 1991

SCM Press
26–30 Tottenham Road
London N1 4BZ

Trinity Press International
3725 Chestnut Street
Philadelphia, PA 19104

Copyright © Jacob Neusner 1991

British Library Cataloguing in Publication Data

Neusner, Jacob *1932*–
Jews and Christians.
1. Judaism. Relations with Christian church, history
2. Christian church. Relations with Judaism, history
I. Title
296.3872

ISBN 0–334–02465–X

Library of Congress Cataloging-in-Publication Data

Neusner, Jacob, 1932–
Jews and Christians: the myth of a common tradition/Jacob
Neusner.
p.   cm.
Includes index.
ISBN 0–334–02465–X
1. Judaism—Relations—Christianity.   2. Christianity
and other religions—Judaism.   3. Judaism—History—
Talmudic period. 10–425.   4. Christianity—Early
church. ca. 30–600.   I. Title.
BM53b.N38   1991
296.3'872—dc20   90–44866

Phototypeset by Input Typesetting Ltd, London
and printed in Great Britain by
Clays Ltd, St Ives plc

Contents

For my dear friends and co-workers at
the Community of Saint Egidio in Rome.
A token of enduring affection and respect.

Preface

While these days Christians and Judaists undertake religious dialogue, there is not now and there never has been a dialogue between the religions, Judaism and Christianity. The conception of a Judeo-Christian tradition that Judaism and Christianity share is simply a myth in the bad old sense: a lie. These essays all together make that single point. Each of the two religious traditions pursues its own interests in its own way, addressing its own adherents with self-evidently valid answers to urgent and ineluctable questions.

True, Christianity and Judaism share some of the same holy scriptures, the Old Testament or the written Torah. But these writings form part of a larger canon, the Bible for Christianity, and the Torah (or "the one whole Torah of our rabbi, Moses," meaning both the parts of the Torah of Sinai formulated and transmitted in writing and orally) for Judaism. Christianity reads the Bible, Judaism studies the Torah. While episodically reaching conclusions that coincide, in general the two religions share no common agenda and have conducted no genuine dialogue. Scripture can provide an agendum—but one that leads only to division, since the Old Testament for Christianity serves only because it prefigures the New Testament, and the written Torah for Judaism can be and should be read only in the fulfillment and completion provided by the oral Torah. To measure the distance between Christianity and Judaism, therefore, you have to traverse the abyss between the New Testament and the oral Torah (the Mishnah, the two Talmuds, the Midrash-compilations). And that has yet to be done, though in the concluding chapter of this book, I shall show how I think we can meet in the middle. As matters now stand, however, it is perfectly obvious that neither religion has a theory of the other framed in terms that the outsider can share, and this underlines the main point: the two religions have not talked and cannot now talk with one another.

That is entirely to be anticipated, given the character of religious traditions as statements, each in its own framework, of the social order. The task undertaken by religious traditions—to account for the social order by appeal to supernatural truth—integrates and excludes, defining the lines of structure and the outer limits as well. So we may hardly expect religions, viewed in this way, to accomplish what to begin with they do not set out to do. If, then, there is to be the dialogue Jews and Christians today desire, it must emerge from a firm grasp of the character of religions, each seen whole and complete as a statement of the social order and a composition of the social system. Then and only then will the encounter begin: the meeting of two corporate bodies, each certain of itself but also engaged by the other, both compelled by shared interests and common tasks.

In these essays I develop these points in three ways. First, in chapters 1 and 2, I underline that from the very beginnings the Judaic and Christian religious worlds scarcely intersected. While commonly represented as an offspring of "Judaism," Christianity in fact began as an autonomous and absolute religious system (or set of systems), only after the fact working out its theory of its origins by taking over and making its own some components of the heritage of ancient Israel. I state this matter in very simple terms: different people talking about different things to different people.

In chapters 3 and 4 I proceed from the first to the fourth century and spell out the occasion on which I think Judaism and Christianity did address a common agenda. But even there, it is clear, no dialogue or debate of any kind took place.

Chapters 5 through 8 turn from historical to theological discourse. I take up the negative and the positive side of the same matter in chapter 5. I argue that there is not now and never has been a Judeo-Christian tradition—a point that Arthur A. Cohen registered with great power in his *Myth of the Judeo-Christian Tradition*[1] and that is now widely accepted, and I proceed to spell out theological reasons for that fact. In chapter 6 I briefly work out one of the fundamental reasons for the lack of dialogue, which is the incapacity of religious systems to think about the other or the outsider—a considerable obstacle indeed.

Chapters 7 and 8, then, mean to point the way forward. The journey will be long and difficult, but if in retrospect I turn out to have shown the way for the first step, that will have been a worthwhile contribution. Only when we recognize difference can we appreciate points shared in common: love of one and the same God, for example; the aspiration to serve and worship that one God; and the absolute requirement, laid upon us all by that one God, to love one another. The "how" of loving one another forms the task of the twenty-first century, but the terrors of the twentieth century have taught us why we must.

The essays gathered here originally served in various contexts, some as addresses, some as papers or essays, some as part of larger research projects. Chapter 3 summarizes my principal statement of the matter, *Judaism and Christianity in the Age of Constantine: Issues of the Initial Confrontation.*[2] Chapter 2 served as a lecture at Pontifical Lateran University in January 1989, and at the National Council of Catholic Bishops, Brasilia, in August of that same year. Chapter 6 was my presentation in Warsaw on September 1, 1989, at the commemoration of the fiftieth anniversary of the German invasion in 1939. Chapter 7 began as an address for the Communità di S. Egidio in Bari, Genoa, Navarra, Naples, and elsewhere; I serve as a kind of rabbi—a teacher of Judaism—for that wonderful group of Roman Catholic servants of God through service to humanity. I express thanks to my hosts on these occasions and also to the original copyright holders for permission to reprint these papers.

University of South Florida,   Jacob Neusner
Tampa

1

Judaism and Christianity

Different People Talking about Different Things to Different People

The earliest Christians were Jews who saw their religion—Judaism—as normative and authoritative. A natural question troubling believing Christians, therefore, is why Judaism as a whole remains a religion that believes *other* things, or as Christians commonly ask, why did the Jews not "accept Christ"? Or to ask the same question in another way, why, after the resurrection of Jesus Christ, is there Judaism at all? Often asked negatively, the question turns on why the Jews do not believe rather than on what they do believe. Yet it is a constructive question even in the context of description and analysis, not religious polemic. For the question leads us deeper into an understanding, not only of the differences between one religion and the other, but also of the traits of the religion under study. In other words, it is a question of comparison—even though the question is not properly framed.

The answer to the question is simple: Judaism and Christianity are completely different religions, not different versions of one religion (that of the "Old Testament" or "the written Torah," as Jews call it). The two faiths stand for different people talking about different things to different people. Let me spell this out.

The asking of the question, why not? rather than, why so? reflects the long-term difficulty that the one group has had in making sense of the other. My explanation of the difference between Christianity and Judaism rests on that simple fact. I maintain that each group talked to its adherents about its points of urgent concern, that is, different people talking about different things to different people. Incomprehension marks relations between Judaism and Christianity in the first century, yet the groups were two sectors of the same people.

Each addressed its own agenda, spoke to its own issues, and employed language distinctive to its adherents. Neither exhibited understanding of what was important to the other. Recognizing that fundamental inner-directedness may enable us to interpret the issues and the language used in framing them. For if each party perceived the other through a thick veil of incomprehension, the heat and abuse that characterized much of their writing about one another testifies to a truth different from that which conventional interpretations have yielded. If the enemy is within, if I see only the mote in the other's eye, it matters little whether there is a beam in my own.

The key is this: the incapacity of either group to make sense of the other. We have ample evidence for characterizing as a family quarrel the relationship between the two great religious traditions of the West. Only brothers can hate so deeply, yet accept and tolerate so impassively, as have Judaic and Christian brethren both hated, yet taken for granted, each other's presence. Christianity wiped out unbelievers, but under ordinary circumstances adhered to the doctrine that the Jews were not to be exterminated. Nevertheless, from the first century onward, the echoes of Matthew's "Pharisees as hypocrites" and John's "Jews as murderers" poisoned the Christian conscience. Jews grudgingly recognized that Christianity was not merely another paganism. In their awareness, however, festered Tarfon's allegation that Christians knew God but denied him, knew the Torah but did violence against its meaning. Today we recognize in these implacably negative projections signs of frustration and anger at someone who should know better than to act as he does, a very deep anger indeed.

The authors of the Gospels choose a broad range of enemies for Jesus and hence for the church. One group, the Pharisees, assumes importance in our eyes out of proportion to its place in the Gospels, because the kind of Judaism that emerges from the first century draws heavily upon the methods and values imputed to the

Pharisees in the later rabbinic literature. So let us narrow our discussion from "Judaism," a word that can stand for just about anything, to that group among first-century Judaisms that in the event contributed substantially to the Judaism that later became normative. And when we speak of Christianity, let us, following the same principle, specify a particular aspect of the rich and various belief of the church represented in the writings of the evangelists. That aspect, the common denominator of the Gospels, finds full expression in the simple claim that Jesus Christ came to save humanity. Hence we shall center on the salvific aspect of the Christianity represented by the Gospels (though not by them alone).

The Judaism defined by the system and method of the Pharisees, whom we meet in connection with the destruction of the Second Temple by the Romans in 70 C.E., addressed the issue of the sanctification of Israel, while Christianity, as defined by the evangelists, took up the question of the salvation of Israel. Both were expressions of Israel's religion; one spoke of one thing, the other of something else. In retrospect, although they bear some traits in common, the two groups appear in no way comparable. Why not? The Gospels portray the first Christians as the family and followers of Jesus. So, as a social group, Christianity represented at its outset in a quite physical, familial, and genealogical way "the body of Christ." The Pharisees, by contrast, hardly formed a special group at all. It is easier to say what they were not than what they were. How so? Although the Pharisees appear as a political group by the first century in Josephus's writings about Maccabean politics, the Gospels and the rabbinic traditions concur that what made an Israelite a Pharisee was not exclusively or even mainly politics. The Pharisees were characterized by their adherence to certain cultic rules. They were not members of a family in any natural or supernatural sense. Their social affiliations in no way proved homologous.

Pharisees, some may object, surely appear as a "they," that is, as a discernible type of Israelite. If they formed some sort of distinct social group, however, and if that group took shape in various places around the country, we nevertheless cannot point to much evidence about its character. We have no documentation of any kind concerning the social traits of the Pharisees as a group.

What we do have is considerable information on certain practices held to characterize and define people who were called Pharisees. If we eat our meals in one way rather than in some other, however, that common practice does not of itself make us a political party or, for that matter, a church: it makes us people who are willing to eat lunch together.

So, as a hypothesis permitting the argument to unfold, let me say that the Christians carried forward one aspect of scripture's doctrine of Israel and the Pharisees another. The Hebrew scriptures represent Israel as one very large family, descended from a single set of ancestors. The Christians adopted that theory of Israel by linking themselves first to the family of Jesus and his adopted sons, the disciples, and second, through him and them to his ancestry—to David and on backward to Abraham, Isaac, and Jacob (hence the enormous power of the genealogies of Christ). The next step—the spiritualization of that familiar tie into the conception of the church as the body of Christ—need not detain us. Scripture, however, did not restrict itself to the idea of Israel as family; it also defined Israel as a kingdom of priests and a holy people. That is the way taken by the Pharisees. Their Israel found commonality in a shared, holy way of life that was required of all Israelites—so scripture held. The Mosaic Torah defined that way of life in both cultic and moral terms, and the prophets laid great stress on the latter. What made Israel holy—its way of life, its moral character—depended primarily on how people lived, not upon their shared genealogy.

Both Christians and Pharisees belonged to Israel but chose different definitions of the term. The Christians saw Israel as a family; the Pharisees saw it as a way of life. The Christians stressed their genealogy; the Pharisees their ethos and ethics. The Christian family held things in common; the holy people held in common a way of life that sanctified them. At issue in the argument between them are positions that scarcely intersect, held by groups whose social self-definitions are incongruent.

Christians were a group comprised of the family of Israel, talking about salvation; Pharisees were a group shaped by the holy way of life of Israel, talking about sanctification. The two neither converse nor argue. For groups unlike one another in what, to begin with, defines and bonds them, groups devoid of a common program of debate, have no argument. They are different people talking about different things to different people. Yet, as is clear, neither group could avoid recognizing the other. What ensued was not a discussion, let alone a debate, but only a confrontation of people with nothing in common, pursuing programs of discourse that do not in any way intersect. Not much of an argument.

Why were the two groups fundamentally different? Why did each find the other just that—totally other? Certainly we can identify groups within the larger Israelite society through whom the Christian familists and the Pharisaic commensals could have come to compare one another. Since the Essenes of Qumran laid great stress on observing cultic rules governing meals, Pharisees could have debated with them about which rules must be kept, how to do so, and what larger meaning inhered in them. Since the Essenes also emphasized the coming eschatological war and the messianic salvation of Israel, Christians could have conducted an argument with them about who the Messiah would be and when he would come. Christians and Pharisees, we can see, bear comparison in an essentially morphological dimension with the Essenes of Qumran. But in the terms I have defined, they cannot be so compared with one another.

Let me answer the question of the fundamental difference between the two religious traditions by pointing out what really does make parallel the formulation of the Judaism of each. I mean to make a very simple point. Christianity and Judaism each took over the inherited symbolic structure of Israel's religion. Each, in fact, did work with the same categories as the other. But in the hands of each, the available and encompassing classification-system found wholly new meaning. The upshot was two religions out of one, each speaking within precisely the same categories but so radically redefining the substance of these categories that conversation with the other became impossible.

The similarity? Christ embodies God, just as the talmudic sage or rabbi in later times would be seen to stand for the Torah incarnate.

The difference? Christ brought salvation, and for the ages to come, the talmudic sage promised salvation.

Salvation, in the nature of things, concerned the whole of

humanity; sanctification, equally characteristic of its category, spoke of a single nation—Israel. To save, the Messiah saves Israel amid all nations, because salvation categorically entails the eschatological dimension and so encompasses all of history. No salvation, after all, can last only for a little while or leave space for time beyond itself. To sanctify, by contrast, the sage sanctifies Israel in particular. Sanctification categorically requires the designation of what is holy against what is not holy. To sanctify is to set apart. No sanctification can encompass everyone or leave no room for someone in particular to be holy. One need not be "holier than thou," but the *holy* requires the contrary category, the *not holy*. So, once more, how can two religious communities understand one another when one raises the issue of the sanctification of Israel and the other the salvation of the world? Again, different people talking about different things to different people.

Mutual comprehension becomes still more difficult when the familiar proves strange; when categories we think we understand, we turn out not to grasp at all. Using the familiar in strange ways was, I maintain, the most formidable obstacle to resolving the Jewish-Christian argument in the first century. Both Christians and Pharisees radically revised existing categories. To understand this total transvaluation of values, let us examine the principal categories of the inherited Israelite religion and culture. Once their picture is clear, we can readily grasp how, in Christianity and Judaism, each category undergoes revision both in definition and in content.

We recall the major trends in Judaism that earlier emerged: priests, scribes, and zealots. To these we now return, remembering, of course, that there were other trends of importance as well. The principal Israelite categories are discernible both in the distinct types of holy men whom we know as priests, scribes, and messiahs, and in the definitive activities of cult, school, and government offices, and (ordinarily) the battlefield. Ancient Israel's heritage yielded the cult with its priests, the Torah with its scribes and teachers, and the prophetic and apocalyptic hope for meaning in history and an eschaton mediated by messiahs and generals. From these derive Temple, school, and (in the apocalyptic expectation) battlefield on earth and in heaven.

To seek a typology of the modes of Israelite piety, we must look for the generative symbol of each mode: an altar for the priestly ideal, a scroll of scripture for the scribal ideal of wisdom, a coin marked "Israel's freedom: year one" for the messianic modality. In each of these visual symbols we perceive things we cannot touch, hearts and minds we can only hope to evoke. We seek to enter into the imagination of people distant in space and time. We must strive to understand the way in which they framed the world and encapsulated their world view in some one thing: the sheep for the priestly sacrifice, the memorized aphorism for the disciple, the stout heart for the soldier of light. Priest, sage, soldier—each stands for the whole of Israel. When all would meld into one, there would emerge a fresh and unprecedented Judaism, whether among the heirs of scribes and Pharisees or among the disciples of Christ.

The symbols under discussion—Temple altar, sacred scroll, victory wreath for the head of the King-Messiah—largely covered Jewish society. We need not reduce them to their merely social dimensions to recognize that on them was founded the organization of Israelite society and the interpretation of its history. Let us rapidly review the social groups envisaged and addressed by the framers of these symbols.

The priest viewed society as organized along structural lines emanating from the Temple. His castle stood at the top of a social scale in which all things were properly organized, each with its correct name and proper place. The inherent sanctity of the people of Israel, through the priests' genealogy, came to its richest embodiment in the high priest. Food set apart for the priests' rations, at God's command, possessed the same sanctity; so too did the table at which priests ate. To the priest, for the sacred society of Israel, history was an account of what happened in and (alas) on occasions to the Temple.

To the sage, the life of society demanded wise regulations. Relationships among people required guidance by the laws enshrined in the Torah and best interpreted by scribes; the task of Israel was to construct a way of life in accordance with the revealed rules of the Torah. The sage, master of the rules, stood at the head.

Prophecy insisted that the fate of the nation depended upon the faith and moral condition of society, a fact to which Israel's

internal and external history testified. Both sage and priest saw
Israel from the viewpoint of externity, but the nation had to live
out its life in this world among other peoples coveting the very
same land and within the context of Roman imperial policies and
politics. The Messiah's kingship would resolve the issue of Israel's
subordinate relationship to other nations and empires, establishing once and for all the desirable, correct context for priest and
sage alike.

Implicit in the messianic framework was a perspective on the
world beyond Israel for which priest and sage cared not at all.
The priest perceived the Temple as the center of the world: beyond
it he saw in widening circles the less holy, then the unholy, and
further still, the unclean. All lands outside the Land of Israel were
unclean with corpse uncleanness; all other peoples were unclean
just as corpses were unclean. Accordingly, in the world, life abided
within Israel; and in Israel, within the Temple. Outside in the far
distance were vacant lands and dead peoples, comprising an
undifferentiated wilderness of death—a world of uncleanness.
From such a perspective, no teaching about Israel among the
nations, no interest in the history of Israel and its meaning, was
apt to emerge.

The wisdom of the sage pertained in general to the streets,
marketplaces, and domestic establishments (the household units)
of Israel. What the sage said was wisdom as much for Gentiles as
for Israel. The universal wisdom proved international, moving
easily across the boundaries of culture and language from eastern
to southern to western Asia. It focused, by definition, upon
human experience common to all and undifferentiated by nation,
essentially unaffected by the large movements of history. Wisdom
spoke about fathers and sons, masters and disciples, families and
villages, not about nations, armies, and destiny.

Because of their very diversity, these three principal modes
of Israelite existence might easily cohere. Each focused on a
particular aspect of the national life and none essentially contradicted any other. One could worship at the Temple, study the
Torah, and fight in the army of the Messiah—and some did all
three. Yet we must see these modes of being and their consequent
forms of piety as separate. Each contained its own potentiality to
achieve full realization without reference to the others.

The symbolic system of cult, Torah, and Messiah demanded choices. If one thing was most important, others must have been less important. Either history matters, or it happens without significance "out there." Either the proper conduct of the cult determines the course of the seasons and the prosperity of the land, or it is "merely ritual"—an unimportant external and not the critical heart. (We hear this judgment in, for example, the prophetic polemic against the cult.) Either the Messiah will save Israel, or he will ruin everything. Accordingly, though we take for granted that people could have lived within the multiple visions of priest, sage, and Messiah, we must also recognize that such a life was vertiginous. Narratives of the war of 66–73 C.E. emphasize that priests warned messianists not to endanger their Temple. Later sages—talmudic rabbis—paid slight regard to the messianic struggle led by Bar Kokhba, and after 70 C.E., claimed the right to tell priests what to do.

The way in which symbols were arranged and rearranged was crucial. Symbol change is social change. A mere amalgam of all three symbols hardly serves by itself as a mirror for the mind of Israel. The particular way the three were bonded in a given system reflects an underlying human and social reality. That is how it should be since, as we saw, the three symbols with their associated myths, the world views they projected, and the way of life they defined, stood for different views of what really matters. In investigating the existential foundations of the several symbolic systems available to Jews in antiquity, we penetrate to the bedrock of Israel's reality, to the basis of the life of the nation and of each Israelite, to the ground of being—even to the existential core that we the living share with them.

Let us unpack the two foci of existence: public history and the private establishment of the home and heart. We may call the first "time." Its interest is in one-time, unique *events* that happen day by day in the here and now of continuing history. The other focus we may call "eternity." Its interest is in the recurrent and continuing *patterns* of life—birth and death, planting and harvest, the regular movement of the sun, moon, stars in heaven, night and day, Sabbaths, festivals and regular seasons on earth. The two share one existential issue: How do we respond to the ups and downs of life?

The events of individual life—birth, maturing, marriage, death—do not make history, except for individuals. But the events of group life—the formation of groups, the development of social norms and patterns, depression and prosperity, war and peace—these do make history. When a small people coalesces and begins its course through history in the face of adversity, one of two things can happen. Either the group may disintegrate in the face of disaster and lose its hold on its individual members, or the group may fuse, being strengthened by trial, and so turn adversity into renewal.

The modes around which Israelite human and national existence coalesced—those of priests, sages, and messianists (including prophets and apocalyptists)—emerge, we must remember, from national and social consciousness. The heritage of the written Torah (the Hebrew scriptures or "Old Testament") was carried forward in all three approaches to Judaism. The Jewish people knew the mystery of how to endure through history. In ancient Israel adversity elicited self-conscious response. Things did not merely *happen* to Israelites. God made them happen to teach lessons to Israel. The prophetic and apocalyptic thinkers in Israel shaped, reformulated, and interpreted events, treating them as raw material for renewing the life of the group.

History was not merely "one damn thing after another." It was important, teaching significant lessons. It had a purpose and was moving somewhere. The writers of Leviticus and Deuteronomy, of the historical books from Joshua through Kings, and of the prophetic literature agreed that, when Israel did God's will, it enjoyed peace, security, and prosperity; when it did not, it was punished at the hands of mighty kingdoms raised up as instruments of God's wrath. This conception of the meaning of Israel's life produced another question: How long? When would the great events of time come to their climax and conclusion? As one answer to that question there arose the hope for the Messiah, the anointed of God, who would redeem the people and set them on the right path forever, thus ending the vicissitudes of history.

When we reach the first century C.E., we come to a turning point in the messianic hope. No one who knows the Gospels will be surprised to learn of the intense, vivid, prevailing expectation among some groups that the Messiah was coming soon. Their anticipation is hardly astonishing. People who fix their attention on contemporary events of world-shaking dimensions naturally look to a better future. That expectation is one context for the messianic myth.

More surprising is the development among the people of Israel of a second, quite different response to history. It is the response of those prepared once and for all to transcend historical events and to take their leave of wars and rumors of wars, of politics and public life. These persons, after 70 C.E., undertook to construct a new reality beyond history, one that focused on the meaning of humdrum everyday life. We witness among the sages ultimately represented in the Mishnah neither craven nor exhausted passivity in the face of world-shaking events, but the beginnings of an active construction of a new mode of being. They chose to exercise freedom uncontrolled by history, to reconstruct the meaning and ultimate significance of events, to seek a world within ordinary history, a different and better world. They undertook a quest for eternity in the here and now; they strove to form a society capable of abiding amid change and stress. Indeed, it was a fresh reading of the meaning of history. The nations of the world suppose that they make "history" and think that their actions matter. But these sages knew that it is God who makes history, and that it is the reality formed in response to God's will that counts as history: God is the king of kings.

This conception of time and change had, in fact, formed the focus of the earlier priestly tradition, which was continued later in the Judaism called rabbinic or talmudic. This Judaism offered an essentially metahistorical approach to life. It lived above history and its problems. It expressed an intense inwardness. The Judaism attested in the rabbis' canon of writings emphasized the ultimate meaning contained within small and humble affairs. Rabbinic Judaism came in time to set itself up as the alternative to all forms of messianic Judaism—whether in the form of Christianity or militaristic zealotry and nationalism—which claimed to know the secret of history, the time of salvation, and the way to redemption. But, paradoxically, the canonical writings of rabbis also disclosed answers to these questions. The Messiah myth was absorbed into the rabbis' system and made to strengthen it. The

rabbinical canon defined in a new way the uses and purposes of
all else that had gone before.

This approach to the life of Israel, stressing continuity and
pattern and promising change only at the very end when all would
be in order, represents the union of two trends. The one was
symbolized by the altar; the other by the Torah scroll, the priest,
and the sage. In actual fact, the union was effected by a kind of
priest *manqué* and by a special kind of sage. The former was the
Pharisee, the latter the scribe.

The scribes were a profession. They knew and taught Torah.
They took their interpretation of Torah very seriously, and for
them the act of study had special importance. The Pharisees were
a sect which had developed a peculiar perception of how to live
and interpret life: they acted in their homes as if they were priests
in the Temple. Theirs was an "as if" way. They lived "as if" they
were priests, "as if" they had to obey at home the laws that applied
to the Temple. When the Temple was destroyed in 70 C.E., the
Pharisees were prepared. They continued to live "as if" there
were a new Temple composed of the Jewish people.

These, then, represent the different ways in which the great
events were experienced and understood. One was the historical-
messianic way, stressing the intrinsic importance of events and
concentrating upon their weight and meaning. The other was the
metahistorical, scribal-priestly-rabbinic way, which emphasized
Israel's power of transcendence and the construction of an eternal,
changeless mode of being in this world, capable of riding out the
waves of history.

We may now return to our starting point, where Judaic and
Christian religious life led in different directions. Judaic consciousness in the period under discussion had two competing but
not yet "contradictory" symbol systems: the altar scroll of the
Pharisees and scribes; the wreath of the King-Messiah. What
made one focus more compelling than the other? The answer
emerges when we realize that each kind of piety addressed a
distinctive concern; each spoke about different things to different
people. We may sort out the types of piety by returning to our
earlier observations. Priests and sages turned inward toward the
concrete everyday life of the community. They addressed the
sanctification of Israel. Messianists and their prophetic and

apocalyptic teachers turned outward toward the affairs of states and nations. They spoke of the salvation of Israel. Priests saw the world of life in Israel and death beyond. They knew what happened to Israel without concerning themselves with a theory about the place of Israel among the nations. For priests, the nations formed an undifferentiated realm of death. Sages, all the more, spoke of home and hearth, fathers and sons, husbands and wives, the village and enduring patterns of life. What place was there in this domestic scheme for the realities of history—wars and threats of wars, the rise and fall of empires? The sages expressed the consciousness of a singular society amidst other societies. At issue for the priest–sage was being; for the prophet–messianist the issue was becoming.

The radical claims of the holiness sects, such as Pharisees and Essenes, of professions such as the scribes, and of followers of messiahs all expressed aspects of Israel's common piety. Priest, scribe, Messiah—all stood together with the Jewish people along the same continuum of faith and culture. Each expressed in a particular and intense way one mode of the piety that the people as a whole understood and shared. That is why we can move from the particular to the general in our description of the common faith in first-century Israel. That common faith, we hardly need argue, distinguished Israel from all other peoples of the age, whatever the measure of "hellenization" in the country's life; as far as Israel was concerned, there was no "common theology of the ancient Near East."

No wonder that the two new modes of defining Judaic piety that issued from the period before 70 C.E. and thrived long after that date—the Judaism framed by sages from before the first to the seventh century and Christianity with its paradoxical King-Messiah—redefined that piety while remaining true to emphases of the inherited categories. Each took over the established classifications—priest, scribe, and Messiah—but infused them with new meaning. Though in categories nothing changed, in substance nothing remained what it had been. That is why both Christian and Judaic thinkers reread the received scriptures—"the Old Testament" to the one, "the written Torah" to the other—and produced respectively "the New Testament" and the "Oral Torah." The common piety of the people Israel in its land defined the program of religious life for both the Judaism and the Christianity that emerged after the caesura of the destruction of the Temple. The bridge to Sinai—worship, revelation, national and social eschatology—was open in both directions.

Thus Christ as perfect sacrifice, teacher, prophet, and King-Messiah in the mind of the church brought together but radically recast the three foci of what had been the common piety of Israel in Temple times. Still later on, the figure of the talmudic sage would encompass but redefine all three categories as well.

How so? After 70 C.E., study of Torah and obedience to it became a temporary substitute for the Temple and its sacrifice. The government of the sages, in accord with "the one whole Torah of Moses, our rabbi" revealed by God at Sinai, carried forward the scribes' conception of Israel's proper government. The Messiah would come when all Israel, through mastery of the Torah and obedience to it, had formed that holy community which, to begin with, the Torah prescribed in the model of heaven revealed to Moses at Sinai. Jesus as perfect priest, rabbi, and Messiah was a protean figure. So was the talmudic rabbi as Torah incarnate, priest for the present age, and in the model of (Rabbi) David, progenitor and paradigm of the Messiah. In both cases we find an unprecedented rereading of established symbols.

The history of the piety of Judaism is the story of successive rearrangements and revisioning of symbols. From ancient Israelite times onward there would be no system of classification beyond the three established taxa. But no category would long be left intact in its content. When Jesus asked people who they thought he was, the enigmatic answer proved less interesting than the question posed. For the task he set himself was to reframe everything people knew through encounter with what they did not know: a taxonomic enterprise. When the rabbis of late antiquity rewrote in their own image and likeness the entire scripture and history of Israel—dropping whole eras as though they had never been, ignoring vast bodies of old Jewish writing, inventing whole new books for the canon of Judaism—they did the same thing. They reworked what they had received in light of what they proposed to give. No mode of piety could be left untouched, for all proved promising. In Judaism from the first century to the seventh, every mode of piety would be refashioned in the light of the vast public events represented by the religious revolutionaries—rabbi-clerk, rabbi-priest, rabbi-Messiah.

Accordingly, the piety of Israel in the first century ultimately defined the structure of the two great religions of Western civilization: Christianity, through its Messiah, for the Gentile; Judaism, through its definition in the two Torahs of Sinai and in its embodiment in the figure of the sage, for Israel. Once they understand that simple fact, Christians can try to understand Judaism in its own terms—and Jews can do the same for Christianity. For they have, in fact, nothing in common, at least nothing in common that matters very much.

2

Judaism and Christianity in the First Century

How Shall We Perceive Their Relationship?

From the Nazi period onward, the Roman Catholic Church has formulated its relationship with Judaism in language and symbols meant to identify with the Jewish people, God's first love. To signal his opposition to anti-Semitism, Pope Pius XII said, "Spiritually, we are all Semites,"; and in the aftermath of the Holocaust, successive popes and princes of the church have claimed for Roman Catholic Christianity a rightful share in the spiritual patrimony of Abraham. The epoch-making position of Vatican II represented only a stage forward in the process of conciliation and reconciliation that has marked the Roman Catholic framing of its relationship with both the Jewish people and with Judaism. As an American, I have followed with enormous pride the particularly sustained and effective redefinition of that relationship, which has had its affect upon the civil order and public policy of my own country. The sages of Judaism define the hero as one who turns an enemy into a friend, and the present century's record of the Roman Catholic Church, seen whole and complete, must be called heroic.

Yet in consequence of that sustained and, I believe, holy work, a theory of the relationship between Judaism and Christianity in the first century has taken shape that has exacted a price in both learning and self-esteem. That theory stems from the correct claim of Christianity, in its embodiment here in Rome, to share in the heritage of Abraham, spiritually to be Semites. That claim in its initial formulation stands before us on the Bible, which is the systemic document of Christianity, and that Bible comprises the Old Testament and the New Testament. In this august body, I need hardly rehearse the simple facts of the formation of the Bible by the church of the second and third centuries—the Christian Bible, the Bible that made Christian the Hebrew scriptures of ancient Israel. When the church fathers took their stand against Marcion and in favor of the Gospels' view of Christianity as the natural continuation of ancient Israel's faith, the fulfillment of ancient Israel's prophecy, they rejected the alternative position, that is, that Christianity was something new, plunged downward from heaven without place, without origins, without roots. Quite to the contrary, they maintained (and so has Christianity ever since), in the line of the apostle Paul, Christianity is the olive branch, grafted onto the tree; Christianity begins with the first man; Christianity now fully and for the first time grasps the whole and complete meaning of the scriptures of ancient Israel. These and similar affirmations accounted for the rereading of those scriptures, enriching the faith of the church with the heritage of the Torah, the prophets, and the writings that, by that time, Judaism knew as "the written Torah." That "written Torah" for Christianity constituted "the Old Testament."

With Cardinal Ratzinger, I maintain that hermeneutics forms a chapter in the unfolding of theology, bearing no autonomous standing in the intellectual life of faith. And the hermeneutics that flowed from the formation of the Bible—New Testament and Old Testament—took the position that Christianity was "wholly other," that is, a completely new and unprecedented intervention of God into the life of humanity—but . . . The "but" stands for the appropriation of the life of humanity from the creation of the world onward, as the evangelists and the author of the Letter to the Hebrews would maintain before Constantine, and Eusebius would maintain afterward. Christianity did not begin with Jesus, whom the church called Christ, but with humanity, with the first man, reaching its fulfillment in Jesus Christ risen from the dead. That position left open the question of the place in God's plan for the Israel "after the flesh" that all of the evangelists and Paul identified as the bearers of the grapecluster and the original children of Abraham, Isaac, and Jacob.

That position also left no doubt as to the autonomy of Christianity, its uniqueness, its absoluteness. Christianity did not suffice with the claim that it was part of ancient Israel or that it had adopted the Torah of ancient Israel. The earliest Christians were not Gentiles who became Jews; they were Jews who thought that their Christianity was (a) Judaism. More to the point, Christianity did not constitute a reform movement within Israel, that is, a religious sect that came along to right wrongs, correct errors, end old abuses, and otherwise improve upon the givens of the ancient faith. Whatever the standing of the old Israel, the new Israel was seen to be the true Israel. And that meant it would not be represented as merely a reform movement, playing the role in the drama of the history of Christianity of the Protestant Reformation to Judaisms' Roman Catholic Church. Christianity was born on the first Easter with the resurrection of Jesus Christ, as the church saw matters. That event was unique, absolute, unprecedented. Christianity did not have to present itself as a reformation of Judaism, because it had nothing to do with any other formation within Israel, God's first love. Christianity was not a Judaism: it was Judaism, because it was Christianity, from Easter onward. So, I think, the church understood, and as part of that understanding, in later times the church gave birth within its tradition to the Bible.

In representing Christianity as a reform movement within an antecedent and an ongoing Judaism, this received self-understanding of the church was set aside. And, I am inclined to think, our century has witnessed a fundamental theological error which has, as a matter of fact, also yielded an erroneous hermeneutics. It is, moreover, to speak plainly, a Protestant error. The theological error was to represent Christianity as a natural, this-worldly reform, a continuation of Judaism in the terms of Judaism. The New Testament would then be read in light of the Old, rather than the Old in light of the New. And that forms the hermeneutics that has predominated. We go to the Judaic writings of the age, or of the age thereafter, to discover the context in which Christianity was born; and Christianity then is understood to be represented by the Bible, or the New Testament in particular: a problem of reading writing, not of sifting through the heritage of tradition that the church conveyed. The theological error of seeing

Christianity as continuous and this-worldly, rather than as a divine intervention into history and as supernatural, affected not only the Christian understanding of Christianity. It also carried in its wake a theory of who is Israel, Israel after the flesh, that contradicted the position of the church before our time.

The church, in the tradition of the apostle Paul in Romans, affirmed the salvation of Israel through the heritage of Abraham and Sarah. But now that "Judaism" that had become Christianity was given an autonomous standing, on the one side, and also assigned negative traits, on the other. Christianity became necessary in this-worldly terms to reform Judaism, and that reformed Judaism defined the theological verities for Christianity. It was a Christian theology of Judaism as an "if-only" theology of Judaism: if only Judaism were done rightly, it would have been (and would be) all right with God. That theology yielded a hermeneutic in which the faults of "the Jews" or of "Judaism" were contrasted with the virtues of Jesus and of Christianity. Judaism–then required reformation; Judaism–now is a relic. Judaism–then bore deep flaws, ethical flaws for example, so that the principal value of Jesus was not as Christ risen from the dead but as a teacher of ethics, as though the Sermon on the Mount contained much that would have surprised informed hearers on one's duty to the other or on the social responsibility of the society. And Christians, for their part, found themselves in a subordinate position in the salvific story of humanity, becoming not the true Israel by faith in Christ Jesus (as Paul would want us to maintain), but merely Israel by default, that is, by default of the old Israel.

The appeal of the Reformation churches, their theology and, consequently, their hermeneutics, to a theory of Christianity as a (mere) reform of Judaism, and of Judaism as hopelessly requiring a reformation, imposed on the state of the first century the world–historical drama of the sixteenth century. In their picture of the founding of Christianity, the Reformation theologians imputed their own situation to that time of perfection that formed the authority and the model. *Sola scriptura* carried with it not only an apologetic for the new, but also a reconstruction of the old; only by reference to scripture shall we know what Christ really had in mind, and scripture, read independent of the heritage of the tradition that the church sustained, meant the New Testament in light of the Old. And that brings us back to our own century, its theology, and its hermeneutics.

The theology that saw Christianity as a reformation of Judaism, so identifying the Reformation as the new and sole Christianity, yielded a hermeneutic that would read the life of Jesus as continuous with the Judaism of his day, and the salvation of Christ as an event within the Judaism of the first century. What that meant is that scholars would turn to the Judaic writings of the time not merely for information about how things were and were done at that time, but for insight into the meaning and message—the religious message, the theological truth of the New Testament. It was kind of a reverse-Marcionism. Instead of rejecting the Old Testament in favor of the New, the hermeneutics that has guided thought on the relationship of Judaism and Christianity in the first century has appealed to "the Talmud," that is, to the literature of the ancient rabbis broadly construed, as the keystone and guide in the reading of the New. The Old Testament, then, would be set aside as merely interesting; salvation would come of, not the Jews, but of the rabbis.

The observation about the current state of New Testament hermeneutics draws us back to the point at which I began, namely, the affirmation of the church as "Semitic"; the declaration, in the very teeth of Nazism, that "spiritually, we are all Semites"; the insistence upon the Judaic heritage of the church and of Christianity. Given the tragedy of Christianity in the civilization of Christian Europe, perverted by Nazism and corrupted by communism, given the natural humanity that accorded to suffering Israel for the first time an honorable place within the faith, we must admire the intent. Everyone meant well, and today means well. But the result is an unchristian reading of the New Testament and, as a matter of fact, a misunderstanding, from the viewpoint of the history of religion, of the New Testament and the whole of the Bible as well.

I have already made clear what I mean by an unchristian reading of the New Testament. It is the hermeneutic that appeals for the solution of exegetical problems to Judaic sources, in the manner of Strack-Billerbeck, for instance. That hermeneutic, I have argued, flows from the theology of Christianity as a continuation of and mere improvement upon Judaism. But if, as

I have pointed out, Christianity understands itself as autonomous, unique, absolute, then Christianity cannot be a mere reformation. And not only so, but if, as we Jews maintain, the Torah of our Rabbi Moses, encompassing both the written Torah and the oral Torah, bears no relationship whatsoever to any other revelation that God may have had in mind; if, as we hold, what God wants of all humanity rests in the commandments to the children of Noah, then we cannot find a compliment in this same notion. We are no relic; ours is not the unreformed sediment, nor are we the stubborn and incorrigible heirs of a mere denial. We bear the living faith, the Torah, of the one true God, Creator of heaven and earth, who gave us the Torah and who implanted within us eternal life: so is the faith of Israel, God's first love. But in the context of this tragic century, we too have found reasons to affirm the picture of the first century as an age of reform, of Christianity as profoundly interrelated with Judaism in the way in which Protestant theology maintained.

The theological error does not dwarf the one that has characterized the historical account of the religions, Judaism and Christianity. The error as to history of religion is distinct. It is in two parts; one theological, the other religious. The theological error concerns history, not belief but (mere) description. As Cardinal Ratzinger warned as to theology and hermeneutics, it too represents a hermeneutical error concerning the reading now of history, flowing from a theological position. The theological error, in this case, comes not from Christianity but from Judaism. It is the position that there was, is, and can forever be only one Judaism, the orthodox one. Speaking from the perspective of Sinai, one surely affirms that view. Translating theological truth into historical fact, however, reduces theology to a matter of description, and that is an error. Consequently it imposes upon history the burden of faith. That is as grave an offense against religion as asking science to conform in its results to scripture in its crudest interpretation. In the case of the first century, we have been asked to see one Judaism, the orthodox one, and to see that Judaism in the first century as an exact representation of what would emerge in the Talmud of Babylonia seven hundred years later. It would follow that if we want to know what Judaism, the one, orthodox Judaism, was in the first century, we have simply to consult the later writings in which that Judaism came to full and complete expression. That orthodox theology of Judaism stands behind the possibility, represented by Strack-Billerbeck, of interpreting the New Testament as an essentially Judaic book, the life of Jesus as the story of a great rabbi, the formation of the church as an aberration, and the work of the apostle Paul as a betrayal, an invention of a Christianity Rabbi Jesus never contemplated—and on and on.

The theological error on the Christian side is to read Christianity as a continuation and reform of Judaism. That makes possible the hermeneutic—supplied by orthodox Judaism, by Jewish apologists, by Christian friends of the Jewish people, by pretty much everybody of good will in our own awful century—that reads Christianity as contingent upon Judaism, secondary to Judaism, not absolute, not unique, not autonomous. The theological error on the Judaic side is to seek in the social facts of the history of the here and now the replication of God's Torah's picture of holy Israel. It was (and is) a positivist conception that the facts of history settle the affirmations of faith, that the sanctity of holy Israel living by the Torah is to be affirmed, because in the first century (first only for the Christians, after all) there was that one true, orthodox, Orthodox Judaism that pretty much everybody affirmed (even Jesus), and that, as a matter of mere fact, Christianity distorted—so runs the apologetic.

I spoke of an error as to history of religion, and in correcting that error, I propose to set forth a constructive program, one that accords with the theological self-understandings of absolute Christianity and unique Judaism alike. Out of the history of religion I want to form the possibility of a new classicism in theology of Judaism and theology of Christianity—no mean ambition. This program aims at allowing Christianity to be absolute, Judaism to be unique, and the two to define for the twenty-first century a shared range of genuinely religious discourse, one to which the facts of history are not critical, but the confrontation with God, central. I wish, in a word, for Judaism to be Torah, the one whole Torah God revealed to Moses at Sinai, not subject to the uncertainties of time or the varieties of circumstance; and I want, for Christianity, that autonomous standing, that confidence that permits the end to the question addressed here, there, and everywhere, why not? (that is, why not become like us?) and permits the asking of the question, how? (that is, how shall we all find, in Christian language, each his or her cross; in Judaic language, each in the face of the other the image and likeness of God?).

No small task, no mean ambition. Where to begin? Just as theology comes prior to hermeneutics, so religion comes prior to hermeneutics. We have therefore, in the realm of history of religion, to undertake first to define what we mean by religion, then to carry that definition onward to the reading of the holy books that concern us. A shift in language is required, however, from "religion" to "religious system." When I speak of "religious system," I refer to the cogent statement, framed in supernatural terms, of a social entity concerning its way of life, its world view, and its definition of itself. When a group of people, whether numerous, whether few, share a conception of themselves as a social entity, when they explain by appeal to transcendent considerations the very everyday pattern that defines what they do together, then the conception they set forth to account for themselves comprises their religious system. In simple terms, a religious system is made up of a cogent theory of ethics, that is, way of life; ethos, that is, world view; and ethnos, that is, social entity.

Religions seen in this way form social worlds and do so through the power of their rational thought, that is, their capacity to explain data in a (to an authorship) self-evidently valid way. As to hermeneutics flowing from this theory of religion, the framers of religious documents answer urgent questions, framed in society and politics to be sure, in a manner deemed self-evidently valid by those addressed by the authorships at hand. Religious writings present striking examples of how people in writing explain to themselves who they are as a social entity. Religion as a powerful force in human society and culture is realized in society, not only or mainly theology; religion works through the social entity that embodies that religion. Religions form social entities—churches or peoples or holy nations or monasteries or communities—that, in the concrete, constitute the "us" as against "the nations," or merely, "them." Religions carefully explain, in deeds and in words, who that "us" is—and they do it every day. To see religion in this way is to take religion seriously as a way of realizing, in classic documents, a large conception of the world.

That brings us to the systemic hermeneutics in the reading of the formative documents of Judaism or of Christianity. Writings such as those we read have been selected by the framers of a religious system, and read all together, those writings are deemed to make a cogent and important statement of that system; hence the category, "canonical writings." I call that encompassing, canonical picture a "system," when it is composed of three necessary components: an account of a world view, a prescription of a corresponding way of life, and a definition of the social entity that finds definition in the one and description in the other. When those three fundamental components fit together, they sustain one another in explaining the whole of a social order, hence constituting the theoretical account of a system. Systems defined in this way work out a cogent picture, for those who make them up, of *how* things are correctly to be sorted out and fitted together, of *why* things are done in one way rather than in some other, and of *who* they are that do and understand matters in this particular way. When, as is commonly the case, people invoke God as the foundation for their world view, maintaining that their way of life corresponds to what God wants of them, projecting their social entity in a particular relationship to God, then we have a religious system. When, finally, a religious system appeals as an important part of its authoritative literature or canon to the Hebrew scriptures of ancient Israel or "Old Testament," we have a Judaism.

We describe systems from their end products, the writings. But we have then to work our way back from canon to system, not to imagine either that the canon is the system or that the canon creates the system. The canonical writings speak, in particular, to those who can hear, that is, to the members of the community who, on account of that perspicacity of hearing, constitute the social entity or systemic community. The community then comprises that social group, the system of which is recapitulated by the selected canon. The group's exegesis of the canon in terms of the everyday imparts to the system the power to sustain the community in a reciprocal and self-nourishing process. The community through its exegesis then imposes continuity and unity on whatever is in its canon. The power of a system to persist expresses or attests to a symbolic transaction. That symbolic transaction, specifically, takes place in its exegesis of the systemic canon which, in literary terms, constitutes the social entity's statement of itself. So the texts recapitulate the system. (In the language of Roman Catholic Christianity, the Bible is the Bible of the church, which is to say, scripture and tradition form the authority and criterion of Christian truth, not scripture alone.) The system does not recapitulate the texts. The system comes before the texts and defines the canon. The exegesis of the canon then forms that ongoing social action that sustains the whole. A system does not recapitulate its texts; it selects and orders them. A religious system imputes cogency to them as a whole, one to the next, that their original authorships have not expressed in and through the parts; and through them a religious system expresses its deepest logic, *and it also frames that just fit that joins system to circumstance.*

The whole works its way out through exegesis, and the history of any religious system is the exegesis of its exegesis. The first rule of the exegesis of systems is the simplest and the one with which I conclude: *the system does not recapitulate the canon; the canon recapitulates the system.* The system forms a statement of a social entity, specifying its world view and way of life in such a way that, to the participants in the system, the whole makes sound sense, beyond argument. So in the beginning are not words of inner and intrinsic affinity, but (as Philo would want us to say) the Word: the transitive logic, the system, all together, all at once, complete, whole, finished — the word awaiting only that labor of exposition and articulation that the faithful, for centuries to come, will lavish at the altar of the faith. A religious system therefore presents a fact not of history but of immediacy, of the social present.

By the definitions just now given, can we identify one Judaism in the first centuries B.C.E and C.E.? Only if we can treat as a single cogent statement everything all Jews wrote. That requires us to harmonize the Essene writings of the Dead Sea, Philo, the Mishnah, the variety of scriptures collected in our century as the apocrypha and pseudepigrapha of the Old Testament, not to mention the Gospels! That is to say, viewed as statements of systems, the writings attest to diverse religious systems, and in the setting of which we speak, to diverse Judaisms. There was no one orthodoxy, no Orthodox Judaism. There were various Judaisms. In that context, the formative writings of what we call Christianity form statements of systems, and whether we call them Judaisms or Christianities really does not affect how we shall read them—*in that context*. For reading a text in its (systemic) context and as a statement of a larger matrix of meaning, requires us to accord to each system, to each Judaism, that autonomy and uniqueness and absoluteness that every Judaism has claimed for itself; and, it goes without saying, that all Christianities likewise have insisted upon.

How does the approach to the study of religion define an answer to the question with which we began, that is, the relationship of Judaism to Christianity in the first century? What hermeneutic flows from the theory of religion I have outlined? Each document is to be read in its own terms as a statement—if it constituted such a statement—*of* a Judaism, or at least, *to* and so in behalf of a Judaism. Each theological and legal fact is to be interpreted, to begin with, in relationship to the other theological and legal facts among which it found its original location. A specific hermeneutics emerges.

Let me speak of both Judaism and Christianity. The inherited descriptions of the Judaism of the dual Torah (or merely "Judaism") have treated as uniform the whole corpus of writing called "the oral Torah." They have further treated Christianity as unitary and harmonious. It may have become this but, in the first century, I think both the founder of this place and his protagonist—Peter and Paul—would have regarded that description as surprising. When we define religion in the way that I have, we have a different task from the one of harmonization. It is the task of describing the Judaisms and the Christianities of the age, allowing each its proper context and according to each its correct autonomy. What of the relationship between (a) Judaism and (a) Christianity? There we have to appeal to Judaic writings where they bear facts that illuminate Christian ones, but we must not then reduce Christian writings to the status of dependence and accord to them a merely recapitulative intent: reform, for instance.

Some facts are systemically active: Jesus Christ rose from the dead. Some are systemically inert: they wrote writs of divorce in the first century; some people observed cultic purity even at home;

they kept the Sabbath. We cannot assign to systemically inert facts an active position that they did not and, as a matter of fact, could not have had; and we cannot therefore frame our hermeneutics around the intersections of facts deriving from one piece of writing and occurring in another, later piece of writing. In New Testament hermeneutics, salvation is not of the Jews, because the New Testament is a component of the Bible, and the scriptures of ancient Israel form the other component of that same Bible: all read as the church has been taught to read them, whole and complete, the story of salvation.

Among the religious systems of the people Israel in the Land of Israel—one of which we call "Christianity," another of which we call "Judaism" (and both names are utterly post facto)—we find distinct social groups, each with its ethos and its ethics, each forming its distinctive ethnos, all of them constituting different people talking about different things to different people. As bearers of the heritage of Israel and the fundament of truth of Sinai, we have therefore to affirm that God works in mysterious ways. We Jews can live with that mystery. That is why the seven commandments to which all humanity everywhere is subject make so much difference to Judaism: it is the theory of the other. God asks that much, and if you do it, you are what God wants you to be—no less, but also no more. Why so much is asked of us and so much less of others? That is the mystery of eternal Israel. We not only live with that mystery, we are that mystery. Can Christianity live with that mystery? I think that with the Christian theology of Judaism that has taken shape in Vatican II and since that time, and in the American bishops' framing of matters in particular, Christianity too says its amen to God's work.

In that context, we now look back at the first century from a new perspective. We understand that Christianity is Christianity not because it improved upon Judaism or because it was a Judaism or because Christians are "spiritual Semites" or (to complete the catalogue) because Christianity drew upon Judaism or concurred in things that Judaism taught. Christianity is Christianity because it forms an autonomous, absolute, unique, and free-standing religious system within the framework of the scriptures and religious world of Israel. It suffices therefore to say that the earliest Christians were Jews who saw their religion, Judaism, as normative and authoritative. That affirmation of self then solves the problem that troubles Christians when they (wrongly) see themselves as newcomers to the world of religion: why Judaism as a whole remains a religion that believes *other* things; why the Jews did (and do) not "accept Christ"; or why, after the resurrection of Jesus Christ, there is Judaism at all. Often asked negatively, the question turns on *why* the Jews do *not* believe rather than on *what* they do believe.

Christians want to know *why not*. To me as a rabbi, the answer to that question is simple: Judaism and Christianity are completely different religions, not different versions of one religion (that of the "Old Testament" or "the written Torah"). The two faiths stand for different people talking about different things to different people. And that explains why Judaism answers its questions in its way and does not find itself required to answer Christianity's or Islam's or Buddhism's questions in the way that these are phrased. Judaism sees Christianity as aggressive in its perpetual nagging of others to accept salvation through Jesus Christ. The asking of the question, why not? rather than, why so? reflects the long-term difficulty that the one group has had in making sense of the other. My explanation of the difference between Christianity and Judaism rests on that simple fact. Each religious tradition talks to its adherents about its points of urgent concern, that is, Judaism and Christianity respectively stand for different people talking about different things to different people.

If we go back to the beginnings of Christianity in the early centuries of the Christian era, we see this picture very clearly. Each addressed its own agenda, spoke to its own issues, and employed language distinctive to its adherents. Neither exhibited understanding of what was important to the other. Recognizing that fundamental inner-directedness may enable us to interpret the issues and the language used in framing them. For if each party perceived the other through a thick veil of incomprehension, the heat and abuse that characterized much of their writing about one another testifies to a truth different from that which conventional interpretations have yielded. If the enemy is within, if I see only the mote in the other's eye, it matters little whether there is a beam in my own. But if we see the first century from the perspective of the twenty-first, that is not how matters are at all.

Now we can affirm what has taken twenty centuries for us to understand, which is that we all believe in one God, who is the same God, and whom alone we serve in reverence. That shared life in God and for God defines the relationship of Judaisms and Christianities, then as it does now. But now, through the suffering of us Jews, eternal Israel, and through the response to our suffering of you Christians, Israel with us, we can see that truth as before we did not and could not. So our awful century has left some good for the age that is coming.

3

The Fourth-Century Confrontation of Christianity and Judaism

I. History and Messiah

In the fourth century C.E., beginning with the conversion of Constantine in 312 and ending with the recognition of Christianity as the religion of the Roman Empire in the Theodosian Code of 387, Christianity reached that position of political and cultural dominance that it would enjoy until the twentieth century. In the fourth century, in response to the triumph of Christianity in the Roman Empire, Judaism as shaped by sages in the Land of Israel defined its doctrines of history, Messiah, and who is Israel. Those doctrines successfully countered the challenge of Christianity from then to the point at which Christianity lost its status as self-evident truth in the West. So the age of Constantine was marked by the interplay of issues as defined in the same way by Judaism and Christianity.

In the context of triumphant Christianity, Judaic thinkers represented in the important documents of the late fourth or early fifth century—the Talmud of the Land of Israel, Genesis Rabbah, and Leviticus Rabbah—sorted out three central questions. Having to do with the meaning of history, the coming of the Messiah, and the identity of Israel, they had long presented points on which each party framed its own ideas. Transformed by the events of the age from merely chronic to urgent and acute issues, however, these matters demanded the attention of the Judaic sages. A debate unfolded in which the issues were framed so that a confrontation of an intellectual character took place: people arguing about the same things, drawing upon the same logic, appealing to essentially the same facts. The issues as framed by the Judaic sages and Christian theologians encompassed precisely the same questions, the modes of argument on these issues followed the same rules of reason and discourse, and the facts adduced in evidence by the two parties derived from a shared core of texts available in essentially the same wording to both parties: an argument, a dialogue, a true debate. The two groups — the authorship behind the sages' documents and three representative theologians (Eusebius in the beginning of the century, Aphrahat in the middle and in the Iranian empire, and Chrysostom at the end) resorted to the same corpus of scripture, framed the issues in pretty much identical terms, and drew from scripture answers and implications that exhibit remarkable congruence to the Judaic ones.

The Issues of the Confrontation in the Age of Constantine

We find in the Judaism of the sages who redacted the principal documents at hand both a doctrine and an apologetic remarkably relevant to the issues presented to Christianity and Judaism by the crisis of Christianity's worldly triumph. A shared program brought the two religions into protracted confrontation on an intersecting set of questions, a struggle that has continued until our own time, originating in the fact that, to begin with, both religions agreed on almost everything that mattered. They differed on little, and so made much of that little. Scripture taught them both that vast changes in the affairs of empires came about because of God's will. History proved principles of theology. In that same Torah, prophets promised the coming of the Messiah who would bring salvation. Who was and is that Messiah, and how shall we know? That same Torah addressed a particular people, Israel, promising that people the expression of God's favor and love. But who is Israel, and who is not Israel? In this way scripture defined the categories shared in common, enabling Judaism and Christianity to engage, if not in dialogue, then in two monologues on the same topics. The terms of this confrontation continued for centuries because the conditions that precipitated it — the rise to political dominance of Christianity and the subordination of Judaism—remained constant for fifteen hundred years.

We know the fourth century as the decisive age in the beginning of the West as Christian. But to people of the time, the outcome was uncertain. The vigorous repression of paganism after Julian's apostasy expressed the quite natural fear of Christians that such a thing might happen again. Bickerman states matters in a powerful way:

> Julian was yesterday, the persecutors the day before yesterday. Ambrose knew some magistrates who could boast of having spared Christians. At Antioch the Catholics had just endured the persecution of Valens . . . and unbelievers of every sort dominated the capital of Syria. The army, composed of peasants and barbarians, could acclaim tomorrow another Julian, another Valens, even another Diocletian. One could not yet, as Chrysostom says somewhere, force [people] to accept the Christian truth; one had to convince them of it.[1]

Although matters remained in doubt, the main fact remains: in the beginning of the fourth century Rome was pagan; in the end, Christian. In the beginning Jews in the Land of Israel administered their own affairs; in the end their institution of self-administration lost the recognition it had formerly enjoyed. In the beginning Judaism enjoyed entirely licit status, and the Jews, the protection of the state; in the end Judaism suffered abridgement of its former liberties, and the Jews of theirs.

From the viewpoint of the Jews, the shift signified by the conversion of Constantine marked a caesura in history. The meaning of history, commencing at creation, pointed for Christians toward Christ's triumph in the person of the emperor and the institution of the Christian state. To Israel, the Jewish people, what can these same events have meant? The received scriptures of ancient and recent Israel—both Judaic and Christian—now awaited that same sort of sifting and selection that had followed earlier turnings of a notable order, in 586 B.C.E. and after 70 C.E., for example. Which writings had now been proved right and which irrelevant? So Christians asked themselves, as they framed the canon of the Bible, both Old and New Testaments. Then to Israel, the Jewish people, what role and what place for the received Torah of Sinai, in its diversity of scrolls? The dogged faith that Jesus really was Christ, Messiah, and King of the world now found vindication in the events of the hour. What hope endured for the salvation of Israel in the future? In the hour of vindication the new Israel confronted the old, the one after the spirit calling into question the legitimacy of the one after the flesh: What now do you say of Christ? For Israel, the Jewish people, what was there to say in reply, not to Christ but to Christians? These three issues frame our principal concerns: the meaning of history, the realization of salvation, and definition one's own group in the encounter with the other.

History and its Meaning

The scriptural record of Israel, shared by both parties to the dispute, took as its premise a single fact. When God wished to lay down a judgment, God did so through the medium of events. History, composed of singular events, therefore spoke God's message. Prophets found vindication through their power to enunciate and even (in the case of Moses) to make and change history. Moreover, history, as revealer of God's will, consisted of a line of one-time events, all of them heading in a single direction — a line that began at creation and that would end with redemption or salvation.

No stoic indifference, no policy of patient endurance could shelter Israel, the Jewish people, from the storm of doubt that swept over them. For if Constantine had become a Christian, if Julian's promise of rebuilding the Temple had produced nothing, if Christian emperors had secured control of the empire for Christ and even abridged long-standing rights and immunities of Israel, as they did, then what hope could remain for Israel? Of greater consequence: Was not history vindicating the Christian claim that God had saved humanity through the suffering people of God, the church? Christians believed that the conversion of Constantine and the Roman government proved beyond a doubt that Christ was King-Messiah. For Israel the interpretation of the political happenings of the day required deep thought about the long-term history of humanity. Conceptions of history carried with them the most profound judgments on the character of the

competing nations: the old people, Israel, and the Christians, a
third race, a no-people — as some called themselves — now become
the regnant nation, the church. We do not know that the conversion of Constantine and events in its aftermath provoked sages to
devote thought to the issues of history and its meaning. We know
only that they compiled documents rich in thought on the subject.
What they said, moreover, bore remarkable pertinence to the
issues generated by the history of the century at hand.

We turn to the substance of sages' and theologians' doctrine of
history as expressed in Genesis Rabbah and in the histories of
Eusebius. The program of the two parties was essentially uniform,
and we can therefore presume that a confrontation of ideas on the
same issue took place. When sages and theologians debated
history, three separate matters came under discussion. The first
involved the identification of important events, things that had
happened that made a difference. The second required discerning
the patterns of events, so raising questions of the meaning and
end of history. The third range of discourse, of course, focused
upon the difference history made, what mattered in history, or in
other words, what history proved.

Christian theologians joined the issue with the claim that what
had happened proved that Jesus demonstrated that fact. The
empire that had persecuted Christians now had fallen into their
hands. What better proof than that. Eusebius, for example, started
his account of the age of Constantine with the simple statement:
"Rejoicing in these things which have been clearly fulfilled in our
day, let us proceed to the account . . . And finally a bright and
splendid day, overshadowed by no cloud, illuminated with beams
of heavenly light the churches of Christ throughout the entire
world."[2] Christians entered the new age, as Eusebius says, with
the sense that they personally witnessed God's kingdom come,
not "by hearsay merely or report, but observe . . . in very deed
and with our own eyes that the declarations recorded long ago are
faithful and true . . . 'as we have heard, so have we seen, in the
city of the Lord of hosts, in the city of our God.' And in what city
but in this newly built and god-constructed one, which is a 'church
of the living God'." Then events that mattered are those that
pointed toward the end result, the one at hand. The pattern of
events presented a more complex exercise, since a great many

matters had to fit into one large picture. The proposition, of course, posed no problem.

The Judaic sages, for their part, constructed their own position, which implicitly denied the Christian one. They worked out a view of history consisting in a rereading of the Book of Genesis in light of the entire history of Israel, read under the aspect of eternity. The Book of Genesis then provided a complete, profoundly typological interpretation of everything that had happened as well as a reliable picture of what, following the rules of history laid down in Genesis, was going to happen in the future. Typological in what sense? The events of Genesis served as types, prefiguring what would happen to Israel in its future history. Just as the Christians read stories of the (to them) Old Testament as types of the life of Christ, so the sages understood the tales of Genesis in a similarly typological manner. For neither party can history have retained that singular and one-dimensional, linear quality that it had had in scripture itself.

For his part Eusebius also began the history of humanity from Genesis. He undertook to describe the history of the world from its very beginnings to its climactic moment in which he lived. Sages in Genesis Rabbah did the same thing. Sages, in fact, had inherited two conflicting ways of sorting out events and declaring some of them to add up to history, to meaning. From the biblical prophets they learned that God made God's will known through what happened, using pagan empires to carry out a plan. So some events formed a pattern and proved a proposition. This the sages did not propose to deny. Also from scripture, they inherited a congruent scheme for dealing with history. This scheme involved differentiating one period from another, one empire from another, assigning to each a symbol, e.g., an animal, and imputing to each animal traits characteristic of the empire and the age symbolized by it. This apocalyptic approach to history did not contradict the basic principles of the prophetic view of events, but expressed that view in somewhat different, more concrete terms. But, as we shall see, there was a separate and conflicting theory of events and how to discern their meaning, and that was the Mishnah's. In due course we shall take up this other approach to deciding which events make history, determining the pattern of history, and finally, undertaking to express the proposition or principle that history proved. For the moment, however, it suffices to make a simple point. Both parties—Judaic sages and Christian theologians—did propose to answer one and the same question: what does it all mean? Specifically, for the age of Constantine, how shall we interpret the momentous events of the day? Which events matter? What patterns do we discern in them? And what, finally, do they prove? These questions elicited answers from both parties, different answers to be sure.

Von Campenhausen characterizes Eusebius's picture of history in this way:

> Christianity was the decisive power behind the moral progress of the world, the crowning consummation of the history of thought and religion, and its prophecies and commandments had become the bases of a program of human renewal. Monotheism and the new idealistic morality, which constituted the heart of the gospel of Jesus for Eusebius, were unable to rule the world from the beginning . . . "life, which was still so to some extent animal and unworthy had to be tamed and molded by the beginnings of philosophy and civilization." When the Roman Empire brought peace to the world and overcame the multiplicity of governments, the hour for the Christian people had come, according to the will of God. . . . God has protected his Church in the world from all the demonic onslaughts of its enemies and has led it to victory and success as the shining light of all people.[3]

So history presents the unfolding of God's will. Like Aphrahat, whom we shall meet presently, Eusebius was a scholar working with facts.

The picture of history drawn by Eusebius laid stress on the divine promise to the seed of Abraham, meaning "all who lived according to the standards of piety that would be reestablished and renewed in the world by the coming of Christ." The Mosaic law then had its place as "prologue to the event which would restore that friendship" between God and man, namely, "the coming of the Messiah." Christianity then was not "the upstart religion . . . but the republication of a standard and a code which long predated the Homeric or Mosaic past." This was addressed to all humanity, and the expansion of the Roman Empire "coincident

with the coming of Christ . . . was no accident but had to be seen
as part of the divine plan long ago revealed in the promise to
Abraham. . . . The increase in Roman power meant an increase
in the potential area of Christian activity." With the conversion
of Constantine, therefore, the church "had at last caught up with
the expanding empire. The growing power of Rome had been
preparing the way to be followed by the spreading movement
of Christianity . . . the fact that [Constantine] had become a
Christian was so extraordinary, so overwhelming in its implications and in its results, that it could be explained only as the
outcome of a specific ordinary ordinance of God."[4] Eusebius had
a very specific interest in the Jews and Judaism, of course. He
wished to answer Jews' objections to the gospel and retrieve the
Hebrew scriptures from Judaism, demonstrating that the Old
Testament validates the New. That accounts for his notion of a
worldwide religion before Moses, a religion now fully worked out
in Christianity. Eusebius gave full expression to the idea "of a
world-conquering Christian civilization."[5]

Israel's sages, in Genesis Rabbah, and Eusebius, the great
church historian, bear much in common. Both went back to the
beginnings. From the history of former times both parties wanted
to draw lessons for present and future history. From the story of
the beginnings of the world and of Israel they sought meaning for
their own times. For that purpose they proposed to identify the
patterns in events that would convey the will of God for Israel.
The issue was the same, the premise the same, the facts the same.
Only the conclusions differed. In the initial encounter in the age
of Constantine, therefore, the Judaic philosophers of history and
the Christians represented by Eusebius conducted a genuine
argument: between different people talking to different people
about essentially the same thing.

It was the Book of Genesis. In looking to the past to explain the
present, the Judaic sages turned to the story of the beginnings of
creation, humanity, and Israel, that is, to the Book of Genesis.
In doing so, they addressed precisely that range of historical
questions that occupied Eusebius: Where did it all start? Both
parties shared the supposition that if we can discern beginnings,
we can understand the end. The Israelite sages took up the
beginnings that, to Eusebius too, marked the original pattern for

ongoing history. Sages, of course, would not have added what to Eusebius was critical: Where did it all start—*now that we know where it was all heading all the time*? Sages could not imagine, after all, that what had happened in their own day marked the goal and climax of historical time. Rome formed an episode, not the end. But, then, sages had to state what they thought constituted the real history of the world and of Israel.

The Book of Genesis became the principal mode of historical reflection and response for the sages of the age. They chose that book to deal in precisely the same manner and setting with exactly the same questions that occupied Eusebius: to understand the (to Eusebius) end or (to sages) critical turning, look back to the beginning. In fact, in the present context of debate, only the Book of Genesis could have served both parties so well. For Eusebius, the end would impart its judgment of the meaning of the beginning: this is where things all along had been heading. For the sages of Genesis Rabbah, the beginning would tell us where, in time to come, things will end up. That is the point on which the parties differed, making possible our reconstruction of their genuine argument within agreed-upon limits.

To place into proper perspective the sages' thought on the nature and meaning of history, as expressed in Genesis Rabbah, we had best begin with a look backward toward the place and meaning of history as expounded in the pages of Mishnah.[6] The Mishnah, promulgated two hundred years prior to the composition of Genesis Rabbah, set forth a theory of how events are to be interpreted and what meaning is to be inferred from them. That theory lay in the background of all thought on the same subject, given the Mishnah's authority in the estate of the sages. Accordingly, we shall not understand what sages accomplished in Genesis Rabbah (and in the other documents of the age) without first reviewing the context in which their thought went forward.

The framers of the Mishnah explicitly refer to very few events, treating those they do mention with a focus quite separate from the unfolding events themselves. They rarely create narratives; historical events do not supply organizing categories or taxonomic classifications. We find no tractate devoted to the destruction of the Temple, no complete chapter detailing the events of Bar

Kokhba, not even a sustained celebration of the events of the sages' own historical lives. When things that have happened are mentioned, it is neither to narrate nor to interpret and draw lessons from the events. It is either to illustrate a point of law or to pose a problem of the law—always *en passant*, never in a pointed way. In the Mishnah's limited rhetorical repertoire, narrative is reserved for the narrow framework of what priests and others do on recurrent occasions and around the Temple. In all, that staple of history, stories about dramatic events and important deeds, provides little nourishment in the minds of the Mishnah's jurisprudents. Events, if they appear at all, are treated as trivial. They may be well known, but are consequential in some way other than is revealed in the detailed account of what actually happened.

The Mishnah absorbs into its encompassing system all events, small and large. With them the sages accomplish what they accomplish in everything else: a vast labor of taxonomy, an immense construction of the order and rules governing the classification of everything on earth and in heaven. The disruptive character of history—one-time events of ineluctable significance—scarcely impresses the philosophers represented by the Mishnah. They find no difficulty in showing that what appears unique and beyond classification has in fact happened before and so falls within the range of trustworthy rules and known procedures. Once history's components, one-time events, lose their distinctiveness, then history as a didactic intellectual construct, as a source of lessons and rules, also loses all pertinence. So working like social scientists, as much as did Eusebius, sages sorted out events and classified them. In that way they looked for points of regularity—lessons, laws, and rules—which would explain and make sense of new episodes. In discovering out of anecdotes a larger system of historical—we would say, theological—laws, sages treated history as the raw material for social science. The parallel to the mode of thought displayed by Eusebius is clear.

To this labor of taxonomy, the historian's way of selecting data and arranging them into patterns of meaning to teach lessons proves inconsequential. For history-writing, by contrast, what is important is to describe what is unique and individual, not what is ongoing and unremarkable. History is the story of change, development, and movement; it is not the story of what does not change, develop, or move. For the thinkers of the Mishnah, on the other hand, historical patterning emerges through taxonomy, the classification of the unique and individual, the organization of change and movement within unchanging categories. In the Mishnah's system, one-time events are not important. The world is composed of nature and supernature. The laws that count are those to be discovered in heaven and in heaven's creation and counterpart on earth. Keep those laws and things will work out. Break them, and the result is predictable: calamity of whatever sort will supervene in accordance with the rules. But just because it is predictable, a catastrophic happening testifies to what has always been and must always be, in accordance with reliable rules and within categories already discovered and well explained. That is why the lawyer-philosophers of the mid second century produced the Mishnah—to explain how things are.

The events of the fourth century directed attention to trends and patterns, just as the framers of the Mishnah would have wanted. But in search of those trends, the detailed record of history—so far as that record made trends visible and exposed the laws of social history—demanded close study. That is why sages' response to the historical crisis of the fourth century required them to reread the records of history, as much as Eusebius resifted the facts of the past. The sedulous indifference to concrete events, except for taxonomic purposes, which was characteristic of the Mishnaic authorship, provided no useful model. Concrete, immediate, and singular events now made a difference.

Like Eusebius, sages turned to the story of the beginning to find out the meaning of the present moment. Genesis Rabbah, a work that came to closure sometime after 400, forms a striking counterpart to the writing of Eusebius for one important reason. Its authors not only lived through that same period of radical political change, but also reconsidered the historical question, and they did so in the same way, by reverting to the record of creation, the beginnings of Israel in particular. Once more I enter the necessary warning: whether sages found themselves impelled to do so by the triumph of Christianity we cannot show. We only know what they did, which turned out to be precisely the same thing that Eusebius did. I see no inherent difference between the inquiry of Genesis Rabbah and the question of Eusebius: what patterns do we discern, now that (from Eusebius's perspective) we know where, all the time, things were heading? Since the method of the two parties proved identical and the sources on which they drew were the same, we may proceed to examine the arguments adduced by parties who, we realize, shared one and the same issue and also concurred upon the premises and the proofs for the propositions that, in the mind of each, would settle the issue. Here, therefore, we see how a genuine and authentic argument could have been carried on by two parties to a single dispute.

In Genesis Rabbah, a commentary to the Book of Genesis made up of episodic comments on verses and their themes, the Judaic sages who framed the document thus presented a profound and cogent theory of the history of Israel, the Jewish people. Let me briefly characterize their mode of thought in doing the work. In contrast to the approach of Eusebius, the framers of Genesis Rabbah interpreted contemporary history in the light of the past, while Eusebius read the past in light of the present. So the Israelite sages invoked the recurring and therefore cyclical patterns of time, finding in their own day meaning imparted by patterns revealed long ago. Eusebius, for his part, stood squarely in the tradition that saw events not as cyclical but as one-time and remarkable, each on its own. So the one side looked for rules, somewhat like the social scientist-philosopher, asking how events form patterns and yield theories of a deeper social reality. The other side looked not for rules but for the meaningful exceptions: what does this event, unique and lacking all precedent, tell us about all that has happened in the past?[7] But the two sides met with a single concern: what do the events of the day mean for tomorrow?

Accordingly, the framers of Genesis Rabbah intended to find those principles of society and of history that would permit them to make sense of the ongoing history of Israel. They took for granted that scripture speaks to the life and condition of Israel, the Jewish people. God repeatedly says exactly that to Abraham and to Jacob. The entire narrative of Genesis is so formed as to point toward the sacred history of Israel, the Jewish people: its slavery and redemption; its coming Temple in Jerusalem; its exile and salvation at the end of time. In the reading of the authors at hand, therefore, the powerful message of Genesis proclaims that the world's creation commenced a single, straight line of events, leading in the end to the salvation of Israel, and through Israel, all humanity. That message—that history heads towards Israel's salvation—sages derived from the Book of Genesis and contributed to their own day. Therefore, in their reading of scripture, a given story will bear a deeper truth about what it means to be Israel, on the one side, and what in the end of days will happen to Israel, on the other. But their reading makes no explicit reference to what, if anything, had changed in the age of Constantine. We do find repeated references to the four kingdoms: Babylonia, Media, Greece, Rome—and beyond the fourth will come Israel, fifth and last. So the sages' message, in their theology of history, was that the present anguish prefigured the coming vindication of God's people.[8]

Accordingly, sages read Genesis as the history of the world, with emphasis on Israel. So the lives portrayed, the domestic quarrels and petty conflicts with the neighbors, all serve to yield insight into what was to be. Why so? Because the deeds of the patriarchs taught lessons on how the children were to act, and it further followed, the lives of the patriarchs signaled the history of Israel. Israel constituted one extended family, and the metaphor of the family, serving the nation as it did, imparted to the stories of Genesis the character of a family record. History–become–genealogy conveyed the message of salvation. These propositions really laid down the same judgment, one for the individual and the family, the other for the community and the nation, since there was no differentiating. Every detail of the narrative therefore served to prefigure what was to be, and Israel found itself, time and again, in the revealed facts of the history of the creation of the world, the decline of humanity down to the time of Noah, and finally, its ascent to Abraham, Isaac, and Israel.

So sages read Genesis as history. It was literally and in every detail a book of facts. Genesis constituted an accurate and complete testimony to things that really happened just as the story is narrated. While, therefore, sages found in Genesis deeper levels of meaning, uncovering the figurative and typological sense underlying a literal statement, they always recognized the literal facticity of the statements of the document.

Once we recognize the mode of inquiry, we ask about the results. What are the laws of history, and more important, how do they apply to the crisis at hand? The principal message of the story of the beginnings, as sages read Genesis, is that the world depends upon the merit of Abraham, Isaac, and Jacob; for its part, Israel enjoys access to that merit, being today the family of the patriarchs and matriarchs. That sum and substance constitutes the sages' doctrine of history: the family forms the basic and irreducible historical unit. Israel is not so much a nation as a family, and the heritage of the patriarchs and matriarchs sustains that family from the beginning even to the end. So the sages' doctrine of history transforms history into genealogy, just as Eusebius's doctrine of history turns history into chronology. The consequence, for the sages, will take the form of the symbolization through family relationships of the conflict between (Christian) Rome and eternal Israel. The rivalry of brothers, Esau and Jacob, then contains the history of the fourth century—from the sages' viewpoint a perfectly logical mode of historical reflection. That, in detail, expresses the main point of the system of historical thought yielded by Genesis Rabbah.

Historical study commonly leads to the periodization of history, the division of time into a number of distinct epochs. That patterning of history and its division into eras, each with its own definitive traits, constitutes one important exercise of historical thought of a social scientific order. Eusebius, of course, understood the importance of periodization. Reading scripture, for example, Eusebius identified a number of distinct periods, each leading to the next and culminating in his own time. A principal mode of explaining the identification and status of Israel, the Jewish people, involved the periodization of history among four monarchies, as specified by Daniel (that is, for Leviticus Rabbah, empires signified by various animals in Leviticus 11 and other texts). Rome then stands as the penultimate epoch; Israel for the end. For the present topic, we consider how the patriarchs, for their part, contribute to the periodization of history—itself a source of comfort to doubting Israel even now. For if there is a well-defined sequence, then we can understand where we are and wait patiently until we reach the next, better age. Time and again events in the lives of the patriarchs prefigure the four monarchies among which, of course, the fourth and last (but for Israel) and most intolerable was Rome. Here (Genesis Rabbah XLIV:XVII) is an exercise in the recurrent proof of that single proposition.

XLIV:XVII.
4. A. "[And it came to pass, as the sun was going down] lo, a deep sleep fell on Abram, and lo, a dread and great darkness fell upon him" (Gen. 15:12).
   B. " . . . lo, a dread" refers to Babylonia, as it is written, "Then was Nebuchadnezzar filled with fury" (Gen. 3:19).
   C. "and darkness" refers to Media, which darkened the eyes of Israel by making it necessary for the Israelites to fast and conduct public mourning.
   D. " . . . great . . . " refers to Greece.
   G. " . . . fell upon him" refers to Edom, as it is written, "The earth quakes at the noise of their fall" (Jer. 49:21).
   H. Some reverse matters:
   I. " . . . fell upon him" refers to Babylonia, since it is written, "Fallen, fallen is Babylonia" (Isa. 21:9).
   J. " . . . great . . . " refers to Media, in line with this verse: "King Ahasuerus did make great" (Esther 3:1).
   K. "and darkness" refers to Greece, which darkened the eyes of Israel by its harsh decrees.
   L. " . . . lo, a dread" refers to Edom, as it is written, "After this I saw . . . a fourth beast, dreadful and terrible" (Dan. 7:7).

The fourth kingdom is part of that plan, which we can discover by carefully studying Abraham's life and God's word to him. The inevitable and foreordained salvation follows this same pattern of historical epochs.

XLIV:XVIII.
1. A. "Then the Lord said to Abram, 'Know of a surety [that your descendants will be sojourners in a land that is not theirs, and they will be slaves there, and they will be oppressed for four hundred years; but I will bring judgment on the nation which they serve, and afterward

they shall come out with great possessions']" (Gen. 15:13–14).

B. "Know" that I shall scatter them.

C. "Of a certainty" that I shall bring them back together again.

D. "Know" that I shall put them out as a pledge [in expiation of their sins].

E. "Of a certainty" that I shall redeem them.

F. "Know" that I shall make them slaves.

G. "Of a certainty" that I shall free them.

Reading the verse as a paradigm for all time, we recognize its piquant relevance to the age of the document in which it occurs. There is oppression, but redemption is coming. The lives of the patriarchs bring reassurance. The proposition is that God has unconditionally promised to redeem Israel, but if Israel repents, then the redemption will come with greater glory. If Abraham, Isaac, and Jacob stand for Israel later on, then Ishmael, Edom, and Esau represent Rome. Hence whatever sages find out about those figures tells them something about Rome and its character, history, and destiny.

So Genesis is read as both a literal statement and also as an effort to prefigure the history of Israel's suffering and redemption. Ishmael, standing now for Christian Rome, claims God's blessing, but Isaac gets it, as Jacob will take it from Esau. While Abraham founded Israel, Isaac and Jacob carried forth the birthright and the blessing. This they did through the process of selection, ending in the assignment of the birthright to Jacob alone. The lives of all three patriarchs flowed together, each being identified with the other as a single long life.

This immediately produces the proposition that the historical life of Israel, the nation, continued the individual lives of the patriarchs. Once more we see that the theory of who is Israel rested on genealogy: Israel is one extended family, all being children of the same fathers and mothers, the patriarchs and matriarchs of Genesis. This theory of Israelite society, and of the Jewish people in the time of the sages of Genesis Rabbah, we note once again, made of the people a family, and of genealogy, a kind of ecclesiology. The importance of that proposition in countering the Christian claim to be a new Israel cannot escape notice. Israel, sages maintained, is Israel after the flesh, and that in a most literal sense. But the basic claim, for its part, depended upon the facts of scripture, not upon the logical requirements of theological dispute. And, we see abundantly, that claim constituted not merely a social theory of the classification of Israel—family, not nation like other nations—but also the foundations of a historical theory of the past, present, and future of Israel.

Sages found a place for Rome in Israel's history only by assigning to Rome a place in the family. Their larger theory of the social identity of Israel left them no choice. But it also permitted them to assign to Rome an appropriately significant place in world history, while preserving for Israel the climactic role. Whatever future history finds, adumbration in the life of Jacob derives from the struggle with Esau. Israel and Rome—these two contend for the world. Still, Isaac plays his part in the matter. Rome does have a legitimate claim, and that claim demands recognition— an amazing, if not grudging concession on the part of sages that Christian Rome at least is Esau.

LXVII:IV

1. A. When Esau heard the words of his father, he cried out with an exceedingly great and bitter cry "[and said to his father, 'Bless me, even me also, O my father!']" (Gen. 27:34).

    B. Said R. Hanina, "Whoever says that the Holy One, blessed be he, is lax, may his intestines become lax. While he is patient, he does collect what is coming to you.

    C. "Jacob made Esau cry out one cry, and where was he penalized? It was in the castle of Shushan: 'And he cried with a loud and bitter cry'" (Esther 4:1).

2. A. "But he said, 'Your brother came with guile and he has taken away your blessing'" (Gen. 33:35).

    B. R. Yohanan said, "[He came] with the wisdom of his knowledge of the Torah."

So Rome really is Israel's brother. No pagan empire ever enjoyed an equivalent place; no pagan era ever found identification with an event in Israel's family history. The passage presents a stunning concession and an astounding claim. The history of the two brothers forms a set of counterpoints, the rise of one standing for the decline of the other. I cannot imagine a more powerful claim for Israel: the ultimate end, Israel's final glory, will permanently mark the subjugation of Esau. Israel then will follow, the fifth and final monarchy.

Messiah

Every page of Eusebius's writing bears the message that the conversion of Constantine proves the Christhood of Jesus: his messianic standing. History—the affairs of nations and monarchs—yields laws of society, proves God's will, and matters now speak for themselves. For Judaism the dramatic shift in the fortunes of the competing biblical faith raised a simple and unpleasant possibility: perhaps Israel had been wrong after all. Since the Jews as a whole, and sages among them, anticipated the coming of the Messiah promised by the prophets, the issue could be fairly joined. If history proves propositions, as the prophets and apocalyptic visionaries had maintained, then how could Jews deny the Christians' claim that the conversion of the emperor, then of the empire itself, demonstrated the true state of affairs in heaven as much as on earth? And as large numbers of pagans and Jews accepted the imperial faith, Christian theologians had also to restate the messianic facts.

Specifically, to former pagans they had to establish the fact that one could worship only Jesus as Christ, no other. To Jews newly entered into the church and to converts from pagan religions, there was another issue. Since the church invoked the Israelite scriptures as warrant for Jesus' messiahship, the standing and status of other statements in those same scriptures required attention. The messiahship of Jesus—so most of the church maintained—rendered void the prior scriptural rules, so that Golgotha did not mark a mere way station on the road to Sinai. If Jesus was Christ, then Sinai (so to speak) had come to Golgotha; converts to Christianity were not to adopt the Old Testament rules and regulations, as the Jews kept them, nor were Jewish converts to maintain the old rites. So for the Christian theologians, the messianic crisis demanded a clear statement of precisely what Christ demanded and did not demand from Christians. Chrysostom, who stands for Christianity in the messianic issue, typifies the Christian theologians' concern that converts not proceed to the synagogue or retain connections with it. The burden of his case was, since Christ had now been proved Messiah, Christians no longer could associate themselves with the synagogue. Judaism had lost, Christianity had won; people had to choose the one and give up the other.

At stake for Chrysostom, whose sermons on Judaism preached in 386 and 387 provide for our purpose the statement of Christianity on the messianic issue, was Christians' participation in synagogue rites and Judaic practices. He invoked the Jews' lack of success in the proposed rebuilding of the Temple in Jerusalem only a quarter of a century earlier, drawing upon the failure of that project to demonstrate that Judaic rites no longer held any power. He further cited that incident to prove that Israel's salvation lay wholly in the past, in the time of the return to Zion, and never in the future. The struggle between sages and theologians concerned the meaning of important contemporary happenings, and the same happenings, read in light of the same scripture, provoked discussion of the same issues: a confrontation.

The messianic crisis confronting the Christian theologians hardly matched that facing the Judaic sages. The one dealt with problems of triumph, the other of despair; the one had to interpret a new day, the other to explain disaster. Scripture explicitly promised that Israel would receive salvation from God's anointed Messiah at the end of time. The teleology of Israelite faith, in the biblical account, focused upon eschatology, and within eschatology, on the salvific, therefore the messianic, dimension. On the other hand, the Mishnah had, for its part, taken up a view of its own on the issue of teleology, presenting an ahistorical and essentially non-messianic teleology. Sages' reponse to the messianic crisis had to mediate two distinct, and I think, contradictory positions. Sages explained what the messianic hope now entailed and how to identify the Messiah, who of course, would be a sage. They further encompassed the messianic issue into their larger historical theory. So we cannot address the question at hand as if the Christians defined the agendum. True, to Israel all they had to say was, "Why not?" But sages responded with a far-reaching doctrine of their own, deeming the question in its Christian formulation trivial.

But the issue confronting both Judaic sages and Christian theologians was one and the same: precisely what difference the Messiah makes. To state matters as they would be worked out by both parties, in the light of the events of the day, what do I have to do because the Messiah has come (Christian) or because I want the Messiah to come (Judaic)? That question encompasses two sides of a single issue. On the issue of the messiahship of Jesus, all other matters depended. It follows that one party believed precisely the opposite of the other on an issue shared in identical definition by both. For Christians, the sole issue—belief or unbelief—carried a clear implication for the audience subject to address. When debate would go forward, it would center upon the wavering of Christians and the unbelief of Jews. Our exemplary figure, Chrysostom, framed matters in those terms, drawing upon the events of his own day for ample instantiation of the matter. The Christian formulation thus focused all matters on the vindication of Jesus as Christ. When Christians found attractive aspects of Judaic rite and belief, the Christian theologians invoked the fundamental issue: is Jesus the Christ? If so, then Judaism falls. If not, then Christianity fails. No question, therefore, drew the two sets of intellectuals into more direct conflict; none bore so immediate and fundamental consequences. When, therefore, Christians in the church of Antioch gave evidence of wishing to join in Judaic worship and practice Judaic rites, with reference to the festivals and the Sabbath, John Chrysostom raised the question of whether Judaic rites yet mattered, and whether Jesus is Christ. So we turn to his framing of matters in our inquiry into the context and circumstance for the Judaic sages' thought on the same topic.

John "of the golden tongue" Chrysostom takes pride of place in the confrontation between Judaism, as represented in the sages' documents, and Christianity, as represented by substantial theologians, because he addressed the issues head on. His principal point was that Christians cannot believe in Christ and also worship in synagogues and observe Judaic rites. Judaism is over, offering no salvation, as the fiasco of the rebuilding of the Temple has proved. In stressing these two points, Chrysostom addressed precisely the issues of the identity of the Messiah and the conditions of his coming that, as we shall see, sages raised in the Talmud of the Land of Israel. Preacher in Antioch, Chrysostom, who was born in 347 and died in 407, addressed the issue of Judaism in a series of sermons in 386 and 387 which accused Christians of backsliding. Not concurring on the honorable title "golden-mouthed," some, represented by Rosemary Ruether, would call John foul-mouthed: "The sermons of John Chrysostom are easily the most violent and tasteless of the anti-Judaic literature of the period."[9] But our point of interest is other than the tradition of anti-Judaism of the fourth-century church, even though that tradition long outlived its original circumstance. What is important to us, as I have already made clear, is how Christian theologians and Judaic sages confronted the issue of who is the Messiah, when he will come (Judaism), or why he will not come again (Christianity)—in all, the shape of the Messiah theme in discourse of the age of Constantine.

The testimony of Chrysostom comes right to the point, because he frames the issue, in fact, as both sides worked it out. For him the principal issue in Judaic "unbelief" and Christian "backsliding" was whether or not Jesus was Christ. If he was, then the Christians should remain firm in the faith, and the Jews should accept it. If not, then not. The issue for Chrysostom carried concrete and immediate consequence: building solid and permanent foundations for the Christian governance. By the end of the century, Christians hardly enjoyed security as the religion of the empire. Julian called into doubt the future of the church in the state, and Judaism remained a vital faith and force. The issue, therefore, proved urgent for political reasons to both Christianity and Judaism. For the one, at stake was the future of a church resting on the messiahship of Christ; for the other, the future of the holy people awaiting the Messiah in the future.

But the specific issue framed by Chrysostom was his own and that of the church. For while the messianic question confronted both sides, each framed the matter in terms of its own distinctive situation. Chrysostom's target was "Judaizing" Christians who attended synagogue worship and observed Judaic rites. Judaism exercised great attraction to Christians, who had in mind to observe Jewish festivals. They attended synagogue worship, resorted to Jewish courts, listened to the reading of the Torah in the synagogue on the Sabbath, and on the next day came to join in the Eucharist. At issue for John was not "anti-Semitism," a wholly anachronistic category. What troubled John was the state of Christian belief. Specifically, John regarded Christian participation in Jewish worship and customs as "Judaizing" or backsliding, that is, an act of disbelief. The backsliders did not believe that Jesus is Christ, and that is why they kept the law, that is, the Torah. Clearly at the heart of the matter was the messiahship of Jesus. All else depended on that question. There was a common and conventional program of rhetoric: the Jews are guilty of "apostasy, faithlessness, rejection of God, and hardheartedness." Jesus had predicted the destruction of the Temple. Not a few years back, the apostate emperor and the Jews had tried to rebuild it. They did not succeed. That proves that the Temple no longer serves to legitimate Jewish religion. All of these commonplaces point to a single issue: was and is Jesus the Christ? That is why Chrysostom plays a part in our invention of a common program of thought for both Judaic and Christian writers in Constantine's age. Since, as Wilken says, "Much of what John says . . . is commonplace," Chrysostom admirably serves our purpose as an interesting and representative figure on the issue of the Messiah, his importance and identity.[10]

Chrysostom's eight sermons, *Adversus Judaeos*, given in Antioch probably in 386 and 387, dealt with Christians who were feared to be soft on Judaism. As a set, the sermons addressed Christians who observe and defend Jewish rites, keep the Passover, and in general, treat the law of Judaism as valid. The response to these views drew upon the exile of the Jews, the destruction of the Temple as Jesus had predicted, and it must follow, the divinity of Jesus. Judaism as such as not the issue; the audience comprised backsliding Christians. The preacher referred to festivals of the autumn season—the New Year, Day of Atonement, and Tabernacles—and he evidently did not wish Christians to keep those festivals, or to observe Easter coincident with Passover. What concerned him transcended attendance at Judaic festivals and fasts. Christians were keeping the Sabbath, attending synagogue worship, and did not know the difference between Christian and Judaic worship. Chrysostom claimed that the Jews' supposed magical power attracted Christians, who went to synagogues for healing. But the main thrust concerned Christ. Jews do not understand the Hebrew scriptures. "The Old Testament was shrouded in a veil, which was lifted only with the coming of Christ," and only by reading the scriptures in light of Christ can anyone understand them.

What is critical to my claim that we deal with a genuine debate on the same issues in the same terms is the argument that the destruction of the Temple and the fiasco of Julian's day discredit Judaism. In Chrysostom's case, the relationship of the destruction of Jerusalem and the divinity of Jesus took pride of place. The longest homily and the most theological-historical, the fifth, is summarized by Wilken as follows:

> the chief topic of the sermon: The greatest proof that Christ is truly God is that he "predicted the Temple would be destroyed, that Jerusalem would be captured, and that the city would no longer be the city of the Jews as it had been in the past." If only ten, twenty, or fifty years had passed since the destruction of the Temple, one might understand doubts about Jesus' prophecy, but over three centuries have passed and there is not "a shadow of the change for which you are waiting" . . . If the Jews had never attempted to rebuild the Temple during this time, one might say that they could do so only if they made the effort. But the course of events shows the reverse, for the Jews have attempted to rebuild the Temple, not once, but three times, and were unsuccessful in every effort. . . . The failure of Julian's effort to rebuild the Temple in Jerusalem, then, is proof that Christ was not an ordinary man among men, but the divine Son of God. His word was more powerful than the feeble efforts of men, for by his word alone he defeated the emperor Julian and the "whole Jewish people" . . . The prophecy of Christ is proven true by the historical "facts" . . . the fulfillment of the ancient prophecies and the continued existence of the church is evidence of the power and divinity of Christ.[11]

And from this all the rest followed. So Wilken concludes, "by keeping the law, by celebrating Jewish festivals, by seeking out Jewish magicians, the Judaizers proclaimed that Judaism was spiritually more potent than Christianity. What greater proof of the truth of Judaism than for the followers of Christ to observe Jewish law?"[12] For Chrysostom at stake was not Judaism but Christianity:

> I ask you to rescue your brothers, to set them free from this error and to bring them back to the truth. There is no benefit in listening to me unless the example of your deeds match my words. What I said was not for your sakes but for the sake of those who are sick. I want them to learn these facts from you and to free themselves from their wicked association with the Jews.[13]

The upshot is that, as Chrysostom framed the issue, everything depended upon the messiahship of Jesus, on the one side, and the confirmation of that messiahship by the events of the age—the power of the church and the humiliation of the Jerusalem Temple, on the other. Everything depended on the Temple, restored or in permanent ruin. Jesus had said no stone would rest on stone, and none did. Julian had tried to rebuild the Temple and had failed. Chrysostom pointed to the Jews' exile as proof of their defeat: "It is illegitimate to keep their form way of life outside of Jerusalem . . . for the city of Jerusalem is the keystone that supports the Jewish rite."[14] The argument recurs throughout the homilies on the Judaizers and forms the centerpiece. No wonder, then, that sages would join the rebuilding of the Temple to the future coming of the Messiah. So the issue framed by Eusebius was carried forward in a logical and cogent way. Sages' response transcended the mere affirmation of the messianic hope. They outlined how to recognize the Messiah and what Israel must do to become worthy of his coming.

In my view the Christian challenge is what stimulated sages' thought to focus upon the Messiah-theme. The Mishnaic system had come to full expression without an elaborate doctrine of the Messiah or even an eschatological theory of the purpose and goal of matters. The Mishnah had put forth (in tractate Avot) a teleology without an eschatological dimension at all. By the closing of the Talmud of the Land of Israel, by contrast, the purpose and end of everything centered upon the coming of the Messiah, in sages' terms and definition, to be sure. That is surprising in light of the character of the Mishnah's system, to which the Talmud of the Land of Israel attached itself as a commentary. In order to understand sages' development of the Messiah-theme in the Talmud of the Land of Israel, therefore, we have to backtrack and consider how the theme had made its appearance in the Mishnah. Only in comparison to its earlier expression and use, therefore, does the Talmud's formulation of the matter enter proper context for interpretation. Critical issues of teleology had been worked out through messianic eschatology in other, earlier Judaic systems. Later ones, as well, would invoke the Messiah-theme. These systems, including the Christian one of course, resorted to the myth of the Messiah as savior and redeemer of Israel, a supernatural figure engaged in political-historical tasks as king of the Jews, even a God-man facing the crucial historical questions of Israel's life and then resolving them—Christ as king of the world, of the ages, even of death itself.

In the Mishnah, ca. 200 C.E., we look in vain for a doctrine of the Messiah. There "messiah" serves as a taxonomic indicator, e.g., distinguishing one type of priest or general from some other. There is no doctrine of the Messiah, coming at the end of time; in the Mishnah's system, matters focus on other issues entirely. Although the figure of a Messiah does appear, when the framers of the Mishnah spoke of "the Messiah," they meant a high priest designated and consecrated to office in a certain way, and not in some other way. The reference to "days of the Messiah" constitutes a conventional division of history at the end time but before the ultimate end. But that category of time plays no consequential role in the teleological framework established within the Mishnah. Accordingly, the Mishnah's framers constructed a system of Judaism in which the entire teleological dimension reached full exposure while hardly invoking the person or functions of a messianic figure of any kind. Perhaps in the aftermath of Bar Kokhba's debacle, silence on the subject served to express a clarion judgment. I am inclined to think so. But, for the purpose of our inquiry, the main thing is a simple fact, namely, that salvation comes through sanctification. The salvific figure, then, becomes an instrument of consecration and so fits into an ahistorical system quite different from the one built around the Messiah.

In the Talmud of the Land of Israel, ca. 400 C.E., we find a fully exposed doctrine of not only a Messiah, but *the* Messiah: who

he is, how we will know him, what we must do to bring him. It
follows that the Talmud of the Land of Israel presents clear
evidence that the Messiah-myth had come that larger Torah-
myth that characterized Judaism in its later formative literature.
A clear effort to identify the person of the Messiah and to confront
the claim that a specific, named individual had been or would be
the Messiah—these come to the fore. This means that the issue
had reached the center of lively discourse at least in some rabbinic
circles. Of course, the disposition of the issue proves distinctive to
sages: the Messiah will be a sage; the Messiah will come when
Israel has attained that condition of sanctification, marked also
by profound humility and complete acceptance of God's will, that
signify sanctification.

These two conditions say the same thing twice: sages' Judaism
will identify the Messiah and teach how to bring him nearer. In
these allegations we find no point of intersection with issues
important to Chrysostom, even though the Talmud of the Land
of Israel reached closure at the same time as Chrysostom's
preaching. Chrysostom dealt with the Messiah-theme in terms
pertinent to his larger system, and sages did the same. But the
issue was fairly joined. In Chrysostom's terms, it was: Jesus is
Christ, proved by the events of the recent past. In sages' terms it
was: the Messiah will be a sage, coming when Israel fully accepts,
in all humility, God's sole rule. The first stage in the position of
each hardly matches that in the outline of the other. But the
second does: Jesus is Christ, therefore Israel will have no other
Messiah. The Messiah will come, in the form of a sage, and
therefore no one who now claims to be the Messiah is in fact the
savior. I can hardly claim that sages went out and bought copies
of Chrysostom's published sermons and composed replies to them.
Issues are joined in a confrontation of ideas, and that is how I see
matters here. The reason is the clear fit between one side's framing
of the Messiah-theme and the other party's framing of the same
theme. And we cannot forget that larger context in which the
theme worked itself out, Messiah joined to the doctrine of history
and of Israel, fore and after, forms a large and integrated picture.
If Jesus is Christ, then history has come to fulfillment and Israel
is no longer God's people. The sages' counterpart system: the
Messiah has not yet come; history as the sequence of empires has

in store yet one more age, the age of Israel; and of course, Israel remains the family, the children of Abraham, Isaac, and Jacob. So Christianity, so Judaism: both confronted precisely the same issues defined in exactly the same way.

In the Talmud of the Land of Israel, two historical contexts framed discussion of the Messiah: the destruction of the Temple, as with Chrysostom's framing of the issue, and the messianic claim of Bar Kokhba.[15] Rome played a role in both, and the authors of the materials gathered in the Talmud made a place for Rome in the history of Israel. They did this in conformity to their larger theory of who is Israel, specifically by assigning to Rome a place in the family. As to the destruction of the Temple, we find a statement that the Messiah was born on the day that the Temple was destroyed. The Talmud's doctrine of the Messiah therefore finds its place in its encompassing doctrine of history. What is fresh in the Talmud is the perception of Rome as an autonomous actor, as an entity with a point of origin (just as Israel has a point of origin) and a tradition of wisdom (just as Israel has such a tradition). So as Rome is Esau, so Esau is part of the family—a point to which we shall return—and therefore plays a role in history. Another point of considerable importance is that since Rome does play a role in history, Rome also finds a position in the eschatological drama. This sense of poised opposites, Israel and Rome, comes to expression in two ways. First, Israel's own history calls into being its counterpoint, the anti-history of Rome. Without Israel, there would be no Rome—a wonderful consolation to the defeated nation. For if Israel's sin created Rome's power, then Israel's repentance would bring Rome's downfall.

The concept of two histories, balanced opposite one another, comes to particular expression within the Talmud of the Land of Israel in the balance of Israelite sage and Roman emperor. Just as Israel and Rome, God and no-gods, compete (with a foreordained conclusion), so do sage and emperor. In this age, it appears that the emperor has the power. God's Temple, in contrast to the great churches of the age, lies in ruins. But just as sages can overcome the emperor through their inherent supernatural power, so will Israel and Israel's God in the coming age control the course of events. In the doctrine at hand, we see the true balance: sage as against emperor. In the age of the Christian emperors, the polemic acquires power. The sage, in his small claims court, weighs in the balance against the emperor in Constantinople—a rather considerable claim. So two stunning innovations appear: first, the notion of emperor and sage in mortal struggle; second, the idea of an age of idolatry and an age beyond idolatry. The world had to move into a new orbit indeed for Rome to enter into the historical context formerly defined wholly by what happened to Israel.

How does all this relate to the Messianic crisis at hand? The doctrine of the sages, directly pertinent to the issue of the coming of the Messiah, holds that Israel can free itself of control by other nations only by humbly agreeing to accept God's rule. The nations—Rome, in the present instance—rest on one side of the balance, while God rests on the other. Israel must then choose between them. There is no such thing for Israel as freedom from both God and the nations, total autonomy and independence. There is only a choice of masters, a ruler on earth or a ruler in heaven.

Once the figure of the Messiah has come on stage, there arises discussion on who, among the living, the Messiah might be. The identification of the Messiah begins, of course, with the person of David himself: "If the Messiah-King comes from among the living, his name will be David. If he comes from among the dead, it will be King David himself" (Y. Ber. 2:3 V P). A variety of evidence announced the advent of the Messiah as a figure in the larger system of formative Judaism. The rabbinization of David constitutes one kind of evidence. Serious discussion, within the framework of the accepted document of mishnaic exegesis and the law, concerning the identification and claim of diverse figures asserted to be messiahs, presents still more telling proof.

Y. Berakhot 2:4
(Translated by T. Zahavy)

[A]   Once a Jew was plowing and his ox snorted once before him. An Arab who was passing and heard the sound said to him, "Jew, loosen your ox and loosen the plow and stop plowing. For today your Temple was destroyed."

[B]   The ox snorted again. He [the Arab] said to him, "Jew, bind your ox and bind your plow, for today the Messiah-King was born."

[C]   He said to him, "What is his name?"

[D]   "Menahem."

[E]   He said to him, "And what is his father's name?"

[F]   The Arab said to him, "Hezekiah."

[G]   He said to him, "Where is he from?"

[H]   He said to him, "From the royal capital of Bethlehem in Judea."

[I]   The Jew went and sold his ox and sold his plow. And he became a peddler of infant's felt-cloths [diapers]. And he went from place to place until he came to that very city. All of the women bought from him. But Menahem's mother did not buy from him.

[J]   He heard the women saying, "Menahem's mother, Menahem's mother, come buy for your child."

[K]   She said, "I want to bring him up to hate Israel. For on the day he was born, the Temple was destroyed."

[L]   They said to her, "We are sure that on this day it was destroyed, and on this day of the year it will be rebuilt."

[M]   She said to the peddler, "I have no money."

[N]   He said to her, "It is of no matter to me. Come and buy for him and pay me when I return."

[O]   A while later he returned to that city. He said to her, "How is the infant doing?"

[P]   She said to him, "Since the time you saw him a spirit came and carried him away from me."

[Q]   Said R. Bun, "Why do we learn this from [a story about] an Arab? Do we not have explicit scriptural evidence for it? 'Lebanon with its majestic trees will fall' [Isa. 10:34]. And what follows this? 'There shall come forth a shoot from the stump of Jesse' [Isa. 11:1]. [Right after an allusion to the destruction of the Temple the prophet speaks of the messianic age.]"

This is a set-piece story, adduced to prove that the Messiah was born on the day the Temple was destroyed; hence, God prepared for Israel a better fate than had appeared.

What matters is not the familiar doctrine of the Messiah's claim to save Israel, but the doctrine that Israel will be saved through total submission, under the Messiah's gentle rule, to God's yoke and service. In the model of the sage, the Messiah will teach Israel the power of submission. So God is not to be manipulated through Israel's humoring heaven in rite and cult. The notion of keeping the commandments so as to please heaven and get God to do what Israel wants is totally incongruent with the text at hand. Keeping the commandments as a mark of submission, loyalty, humility before God is the rabbinic system of salvation. So Israel does not save itself. Israel never controls its own destiny either on earth or in heaven. The only choice is whether to cast one's fate into the hands of cruel, deceitful men, or to trust in the living God of mercy and love. We now understand the stress on the centrality of hope. Hope signifies patient acceptance of God's rule, and as an attitude of mind and heart, it is the ideal action that Israel can sustain on its own as well.

We shall now see how this critical position—that Israel's task is humble acceptance of God's rule—is spelled out in the setting of discourse about the Messiah in the Talmud of the Land of Israel. Bar Kokhba weighs in the balance against the sage, much as the Roman emperor weighs in the balance against the sage, and for the same reason. The one represents arrogance; the other, humility. Bar Kokhba, above all, exemplified arrogance against God. He lost the war because of that arrogance. In particular, he ignored the authority of sages—a point not to be missed, since it forms the point of critical tension of the tale:

Y. Taanit 4:5

[J]   Said R. Yohanan, "Upon orders of Caesar Hadrian, they killed eight hundred thousand in Betar."

[K]   Said R. Yohanan, "There were eighty thousand pairs of trumpeteers surrounding Betar. Each one was in charge of a number of troops. Ben Kozeba was there and he had two hundred thousand troops who, as a sign of loyalty, had cut off their little fingers.

[L]   "Sages sent word to him, 'how long are you going to turn Israel into a maimed people?'

[M]   "He said to them, 'How otherwise is it possible to test them?'

[N]   "They replied to him, 'Whoever cannot uproot a cedar of Lebanon while riding on his horse will not be inscribed on your military rolls.'

[O]   "So there were two hundred thousand who qualified in one way, and another two hundred thousand who qualified in another way."

[P]   When he would go forth to battle, he would say, "Lord of the world! Do not help and do not hinder us! 'Hast thou not rejected us, O God? Thou dost not go forth, O God, with our armies'" [Ps. 60:10].

[Q]   Three and a half years did Hadrian besiege Betar.

[R]   R. Eleazar of Modiin would sit on sackcloth and ashes and pray every day, saying "Lord of the ages! Do not judge in accord with strict judgment this day! Do not judge in accord with strict judgment this day!"

[S]   Hadrian wanted to go to him. A Samaritan said to him, "Do not go to him until I see what he is doing, and so hand over the city [of Betar] to you [make peace . . . for you]."

[T]   He got into the city through a drain pipe. He went and found R. Eleazar of Modiin standing and praying. He pretended to whisper something into his ear.

[U]   The townspeople saw [the Samaritan] do this and brought him to Ben Kozeba. They told him, "We saw this man having dealings with your friend."

[V]   [Bar Kokhba] said to him, "What did you say to him, and what did he say to you?"

[W]   He said to [the Samaritan], "If I tell you, then the king will kill me, and if I do not tell you, then you will kill me. It is better that the king kill me, and not you."

[X]   [Eleazar] said to me, 'I should hand over my city' ['I shall make peace . . . ']"

[Y]   He turned to R. Eleazar of Modiin. He said to him, "What did this Samaritan say to you?"

[Z]   He replied, "Nothing."

[AA] He said to him, "What did you say to him?"

[BB] He said to him, "Nothing."

[CC] [Ben Kozeba] gave [Eleazar] one good kick and killed him.

[DD] Forthwith an echo came forth and proclaimed the following verse:

[EE] "Woe to my worthless shepherd, who deserts the flock! May the sword smite his arm and his right eye! Let his arm be wholly withered, his right eye utterly blinded!" [Zech. 11:17].

[FF] "You have murdered R. Eleazar of Modiin, the right arm of all Israel, and their right eye. Therefore may the right arm of that man wither, may his right eye be utterly blinded!"

[GG] Forthwith Betar was taken, and Ben Kozeba was killed.

We notice two complementary themes. First, Bar Kokhba treats heaven with arrogance, asking God merely to keep out of the way. Second, he treats an especially revered sage with a parallel arrogance. The sage had the power to preserve Israel. Bar Kokhba destroyed Israel's one protection. The result was inevitable.

The Messiah will come any day that Israel makes it possible. Let me underline the most important statement of this large conception:

If all Israel will keep a single sabbath in the proper (rabbinic) way, the Messiah will come. If all Israel will repent for one day, the Messiah will come. "Whenever you want . . . ," the Messiah will come.

Now, two things are happening here. First, the system of religious observance, including study of Torah, is explicitly invoked as having salvific power. Second, the persistent hope of the people for the coming of the Messiah is linked to the system of rabbinic observance and belief. In this way, the austere program of the Mishnah develops in a different direction, with no trace of a promise that the Messiah will come if and when the system is fully realized. Here a teleology lacking all eschatological dimension gives way to an explicitly messianic statement that the purpose of the law is to attain Israel's salvation: "If you want it, God wants it too." The one thing Israel commands is its own heart; the power it yet exercises is the power to repent. These suffice. The entire history of humanity will respond to Israel's will, to what happens in Israel's heart and soul. With the Temple in ruins, repentance can take place only within the heart and mind.

We should not overlook also a corollary to the doctrine at hand, which carries to the second point of interest, the Messiah. Israel may contribute to its own salvation by the right attitude and the right deed. But Israel bears responsibility for its present condition. So what Israel does makes history. Any account of the Messiah-doctrine of the Talmud of the Land of Israel must lay appropriate stress on that conviction: Israel makes its own history, therefore shapes its own destiny. This lesson, sages maintained, derives from the very condition of Israel even then, its suffering and its despair. How so? History taught moral lessons. Historical events entered into the construction of a teleology for the Talmud of the Land of Israel's system of Judaism as a whole. What the law demanded reflected the consequences of wrongful action on the part of Israel. So, again, Israel's own deeds defined the events of history.

The paradox of the Talmud of the Land of Israel's system of history and Messiah lies in the fact that Israel can free itself of control by other nations only by humbly agreeing to accept God's rule. The nations—Rome—rest on one side of the balance, while God rests on the other. Israel must then choose between them. In the Talmud's theory of salvation, therefore, the framers provided Israel with an account of how to overcome the unsatisfactory circumstances of an unredeemed present so as to accomplish the movement from here to the much-desired future. When the Talmud's authorities present statements on the promise of the law for those who keep it, therefore, they provide glimpses of the goal of the system as a whole. These invoked the primacy of the rabbi and the legitimating power of the Torah, and in those two components of the system we find the principles of the messianic doctrine. And these bring us back to the argument with Christ triumphant, as the Christians perceived him. For the important fact is that the Talmud of the Land of Israel expressly links salvation to keeping the law. In the opposite way, so did Chrysostom. We recall that he held that not keeping the law showed that the Messiah had come, and Israel's hope was finally defeated. Sages maintained that keeping the law now signified keeping the faith: the act of hope. This means that the issues of the law were drawn upward into the highest realm of Israelite consciousness. Keeping the law in the right way is represented as not merely right or expedient. It is the way to bring the Messiah, the son of David.

The advent of the Messiah will not be heralded by the actions of a pagan or of a Christian king. Whoever relies upon the salvation of a Gentile is going to be disappointed. Israel's salvation depends wholly upon Israel itself. Two things follow. First, as we saw, the Jews were made to take up the burden of guilt for their own sorry situation. Second, they also gained responsibility for and power over their fate. They could do something about salvation, just as their sins had brought about their tragedy. This old, familiar message, in no way particular to the Talmud's bureaucrats, took on specificity and concreteness in the context of the Talmud, which offered a rather detailed program for reform and regeneration. The message to a disappointed generation, attracted to the kin–faith with its now-triumphant messianic fulfillment, and fearful of its own fate in an age of violent attacks upon the synagogue buildings and faithful alike, was stern. But it also promised strength to the weak and hope to the despairing. No one could be asked to believe that the Messiah would come very soon. The events of the day testified otherwise. So the counsel of the Talmud's sages was patience and consequential deeds. People could not hasten things, but they could do something. The duty of Israel, in the meantime, was to accept the sovereignty of heavenly government.

To conclude, let us ask Chrysostom and the framers of the Talmud of the Land of Israel to take up the same issue.

Will there be a Messiah for Israel?

Sages: yes.

Chrysostom: no.

Will the Messiah save the world, including Israel?

Sages: yes, in the future.

Chrysostom: he already has.

If we ask whether or not the parties to the dispute invoke the same facts, in the form of a shared corpus of texts, the answer is affirmative. The messianic texts of Isaiah and other passages, important to Christians, gain a distinctive reading on the part of sages as well. So the issue is shared, the probative facts a point of agreement. True, Chrysostom and the authors and framers of the Yerushalmi in no way confront the viewpoints of one another. But they do argue about the same matter and invoke the same considerations: is the Messiah coming or has he come? Must we now keep the law or not? The linking of Messiah to the keeping of the Torah joins the two sides in a single debate. To be sure, Chrysostom's framing of the messianic issue responds to concerns of the church and the young presbyter's worry for its future. That is why the matter of the keeping of the law forms the centerpiece of his framing of the messianic question. But the issue of keeping the laws of the Torah then joins his version of the Messiah-theme with that of sages. Again, everything we hear from sages turns inward upon Israel. There is no explicit confrontation with the outside world: with the Christian emperor, with the figure of Christ enthroned. It is as if nothing has happened to demand attention. Yet the stress for sages is on the centrality of the keeping of the laws of the Torah in the messianic process. Keep the law and the Messiah will come. This forms an exact reply to Chrysostom's doctrine: do not keep the law, for the Messiah has come.

4

The Fourth-Century Confrontation of Christianity and Judaism

II. Who Is Israel? The Aftermath

Who Is Israel?

The legacy of ancient Israel consisted not only of scriptures but also of a paramount social category, Israel, God's people and first love. From its origins in the first century, the church confronted the task of situating itself in relationship to "Israel," and Paul's profound reflections in Romans constitute only one among many exercises in responding to that question. For the society of the church, like the society of the Jews, required a metaphor by which to account for itself. And revering the scriptures, each group found in "Israel" the metaphor to account for its existence as a distinct social entity. It follows that within the issue, Who is Israel? we discern how two competing groups framed theories, each of itself and also of the other. We therefore confront issues of the identity of a given corporate society as these were spelled out in debates about salvation. The salvific framing of the issue of social definition—who is Israel today (for Judaism)? what sort of social group is the church (for Christianity)?—served both parties.

We deal with a debate on a single issue. It finds its cogency in the common premise of the debate on who is Israel. The shared supposition concerned God's favor and choice of a given entity, one that was sui generis among the social groups of humanity. Specifically, both parties concurred that God did favor and therefore make use of one group and not another. So they could undertake a meaningful debate on the identity of that group. The debate gained intensity because of a further peculiarity of the discourse between these two groups, but no others of the day. Both concurred that the group chosen by God would bear the name, Israel. God's choice among human societies would settle the question of which nation God loves and favors. Jews saw themselves as "Israel today" joined in the flesh to the Israel of the scriptural record. Christians explained themselves as the Israel formed just now, in recent memory, even in the personal experience of the living, among those saved by faith in God's salvation afforded by the resurrection of Jesus Christ. We therefore must not miss the powerful social and political message conveyed by what appear to be statements of a narrowly theological character about salvation and society. In these statements on who is Israel, the parties to the debate chose to affirm each its own unique legitimacy and to deny the other's right to endure at all as a social and national entity.

But both parties shared common premises as to definitions of issues and facts to settle the question. They could mount a sustained argument between themselves because they talked about the same thing, invoked principles of logic in common, and shared the definition of the pertinent facts. They differed only as to the outcome.

Let us turn to the articulation of the question at hand. The issue of who is Israel, articulated in theological and not political terms, covers several topics: are the Jews today "Israel" of ancient times? Was and is Jesus the Christ? If so, who are the Christians, both on their own and also in relationship to ancient Israel? These questions scarcely can be kept distinct from one another. All of them cover the ground we have already traversed concerning the meaning of history and the identity of the Messiah.

First, was and is Jesus the Christ? If so, then the Jews who rejected him enjoyed no share in the salvation at hand. If not, then they did. The Christian challenge comes first. If Jesus was and is Christ, then Israel "after the flesh" no longer enjoys the status of the people who bear salvation. Salvation has come, and Israel "after the flesh" has denied it. If he is Christ, then what is the status of those—whether Jews or Gentiles—who did accept him? They have received the promises of salvation and their fulfillment. The promises to Israel have been kept for them. Then there is a new Israel, one that is formed of the saved, as the prophets had said in ancient times that Israel would be saved.

A further issue that flowed from the first—the rejection of Jesus as Christ—concerns the status of Israel, the Jewish people, now and in time to come. Israel after the flesh, represented from the Gospels forward as the people that rejected Jesus as Christ and participated in his crucifixion, claims to be the family of Abraham, Isaac, Jacob. Then further questions arise. First, does Israel today continue the Israel of ancient times? Israel maintains that Israel now continues in a physical and spiritual way the life of Israel then. Second, will the promises of the prophets to Israel afford salvation for Israel in time to come? Israel "after the flesh" awaits the fulfillment of the prophetic promise of salvation. Clearly, a broad range of questions demanded sorting out. But the questions flow together into a single issue, faced in common. The Christian position on all these questions came to expression in a single negative: no, Israel today does not continue the Israel of old; no, the ancient promises will not again bear salvation because they have already been kept; no, the Israel that declines to accept Jesus' claim to be the Christ is a no-people.

The response of Israel's sages to these same questions proves equally unequivocal. Yes, the Messiah will come in time to come; yes, he will come to Israel of today, which indeed continues the Israel of old. So the issue is squarely and fairly joined. Who is Israel raises a question that stands second in line to the messianic one, with which we have already dealt. The further question of who are the Christians requires close attention to that same messianic question. So, as is clear, the initial confrontation generated a genuine argument on the status and standing before God of Israel "after the flesh," the Jewish people. And that argument took on urgency because of the worldly, political triumph of Christianity in Rome, joined (as the fourth century wore on) by the worldly, political decline in the rights and standing of Israel, the Jewish people.

Before Christianity had addressed the issue of who the Christians were, Paul had already asked what the Jews were not. Christians formed the true people of God.[1] So the old and lasting

Israel, the Jewish people, did not. Paul had called into question "Israel's status as God's chosen people," because (in Reuther's words) "Israel had failed in its pursuit of righteousness based on the Torah . . . had been disobedient . . . [so that] the privileged relation to God provided by the Mosaic covenant has been permanently revoked." So from its origins, Christianity had called into question Israel's former status, and as Gager says, held that "Israel's disobedience is not only not accidental to God's plan of salvation, it has become an essential part of its fulfillment." The Christian position on one side of the matter of who is Israel, namely, who is not Israel, had reached a conclusion before the other aspect of the matter — the Christians' status as a new Israel — came to full expression.[2]

That matter of status closely follows the issue of salvation, as we have already noted. As soon as Christians coalesced into groups, they asked themselves what *sort* of groups they formed. They, in fact, maintained several positions. First, they held that they were a people, enjoying the status of the Jewish people, and that, as Harnack says, "furnished adherents of the new faith with a political and historical self-consciousness." So they were part of Israel and continued the Israel of ancient times, not a new group but a very old one. But they further defined themselves as not only a new people, but a new *type* of group, recognizing no taxonomic counterpart in the existing spectrum of human societies, peoples, or nations. The claims of the Christians varied according to circumstance. Harnack summarizes matters in a passage of stunning acuity:

> Was the cry raised, "You are renegade Jews" — the answer came, "We are the community of the Messiah, and therefore the true Israelites." If people said, "You are simply Jews," the reply was, "We are a new creation and a new people." If, again, they were taxed with their recent origin and told that they were but of yesterday, they retorted, "We only seem to be the younger People; from the beginning we have been latent; we have always existed, previous to any other people; we are the original people of God." If they were told, "You do not deserve to live," the answer ran, "We would die to live, for we are citizens of the world to come, and sure that we shall rise again."[3]

These reflections on the classification of the new group—superior to the old, sui generis, and whatever the occasion of polemic requires the group to be—fill the early Christian writings. In general there were three: Greeks or Gentiles, Jews, and the Christians as the new people.

When Christians asked themselves what sort of group they formed, they answered that they constituted a new group, and a group of a new type altogether. They identified with the succession to Israel after the flesh, with Israel after the spirit, with a group lacking all parallel or precedent, with God-fearers and law-keepers before Judaism was given at Sinai. The dilemma comes to expression in Eusebius:

In the oracles directed to Abraham, Moses himself writes prophetically how in the times to come the descendants of Abraham, not only his Jewish seed but all the tribes and all the nations of the earth, will be deemed worthy of divine praise because of a common manner of worship like that of Abraham. . . . How could all the nations and tribes of the earth be blessed in Abraham if no relationship of either a spiritual or a physical nature existed between them? . . . How therefore could men reared amid an animal existence . . . be able to share in the blessings of the godly, unless they abandoned their savage ways and sought to participate in a life of piety like that of Abraham? . . . Now Moses lived after Abraham, and he gave the Jewish race a certain corporate status which was based upon the laws provided by him. If the laws he established were the same as those by which godly men were guided before his time, if they were capable of being adopted by all peoples so that all the tribes and nations of the earth could worship God in accordance with the Mosaic enactments, one could say that the oracles had foretold that because of Mosaic laws men of every nation would worship God and live according to Judaism. . . . However since the Mosaic enactments did not apply to other peoples but to the Jews alone . . . a different way, a way distinct from the law of Moses, needed to be established, one by which the nations of all the earth might live as Abraham had so that they could receive an equal share of blessing with him.[4]

Since, with the advent of Constantine, a political dimension served to take the measure of the Christian polity, we have to ask about the political consciousness of the church in its original formulation. In this matter Harnack points out that the political consciousness of the church rests on three premises: first, the political element in the Jewish apocalyptic; second, the movement of the gospel to the Greeks; and third, the ruin of Jerusalem and the end of the Jewish state. He says, "The first of these elements stood in antithesis to the others, so that in this way the political consciousness of the church came to be defined in opposite directions and had to work itself out of initial contradictions."[5] From early times, Harnack says, the Christians saw Christianity as "the central point of humanity as the field of political history as well as its determining factor." That had been the Jews' view of themselves. With Constantine the corresponding Christian conception matched reality.

Now the Christians formed a new people, a third race. When the change came, with the Christianization of the empire at the highest levels of government, the new people, the third race, had to frame a position and policy about the old people, enduring Israel "after the flesh." And, for its part, the Jewish people, faced with the Christian *défi*, found the necessity to reaffirm its enduring view of itself, now however, in response to a pressure without precedent in its long past. The claim of the no-people that the now and enduring Israel is the no-people, knew no prior equivalent. The age of Constantine marked the turning of the world: all things were upside down. How should one deal with a world that (from the perspective of Israel, the Jewish people) had gone mad? Israel's answer, which we shall reach in due course, proves stunningly apropos: right to the issue, in precisely the terms of the issue. But first let us see how a substantial Christian theologian phrases the matter in the polemic at hand.

To show us how a fourth-century Christian theologian addressed the question at hand, namely, who is Israel in the light of the salvation of Jesus Christ, we turn to Aphrahat, a Christian monk in Mesopotamia, ca. 300–350, who wrote, in Syriac, a sustained treatise on the relationship of Christianity and Judaism. His demonstrations, written in 337–344, take up issues facing the Syriac speaking church in the Iranian Empire. The church then was suffering severe persecution on the part of the government, for the monks and nuns, maintaining they had no property, could not pay taxes. Since at that time Jews enjoyed stable and peaceful relationships with the Iranian government while Christians did not, the contrast between weak Christianity and secure Judaism required attention as well. Aphrahat presents his case on the basis of historical facts shared in common by both parties to the debate, Judaism and Christianity, that is, facts of scripture. He rarely cites the New Testament in his demonstrations on Judaism. Moreover, when he cites the Hebrew scriptures, he ordinarily refrains from fanciful or allegoristic reading of them, but like the rabbis with whom Jerome dealt, stressed that his interpretation rested solely on the plain, obvious, factual meaning at hand. His arguments thus invoked rational arguments and historical facts: this is what happened, this is what it means. Scriptures therefore present facts on which all parties concur. Then the argument goes forward on a common ground of shared reason and mutually-agreed-upon facts. Still more important, the program of argument — is Israel, the Jewish people, going to be saved in the future, along with the issue of the standing and status of the Christian people — likewise follows points important to both parties.

Here, as I claimed at the outset, we find Judaic and Christian thinkers disagreeing on a common set of propositions: who is Israel? Will Israel be saved in the future, or have the prophetic promises already been kept? We take up Aphrahat's explanation of "the people which is of the peoples," the people "which is no people," and then proceed to his address to Israel after the flesh. The two issues complement one another. Once the new people formed out of the peoples enters the status of Israel, then the old Israel loses that status. And how to express that judgment? By denying the premise of the life of Israel after the flesh that salvation for the people of God would come in future time. If enduring Israel would never enjoy salvation, then Israel had no reason to exist: that is the premise of the argument framed on behalf of the people that had found its reason to exist (from its perspective) solely in its salvation by Jesus Christ. So what explained to the Christian community how that community had come into being also accounted, for that same community, for the (anticipated) disappearance of the nation that had rejected that very same nation-creating event.

Let me point to Aphrahat's *Demonstration Sixteen*, "On the Peoples which are in the Place of the People." Aphrahat's message is this: The people Israel was rejected, and the peoples took their place. Israel repeatedly was warned by the prophets, but to no avail, so God abandoned them and replaced them with the Gentiles. Scripture frequently refers to the Gentiles as "Israel." The vocation of the peoples was prior to that of the people of Israel, and from of old, whoever from among the people was pleasing to God was more justified than Israel: Jethro, the Gibeonites, Rahab, Ebedmelech the Ethiopian, Uriah the Hittite. By means of the Gentiles, God provoked Israel.

First, Aphrahat maintains, "The peoples which were of all languages were called first, before Israel, to the inheritance of the Most High, as God said to Abraham, 'I have made you the father of a multitude of peoples' (Gen. 17:5). Moses proclaimed, saying, 'The peoples will call to the mountain, and there will they offer sacrifices of righteousness' (Deut. 33:19)." Not only so, but God further rejected Israel: "To his people Jeremiah preached, saying to them, 'Stand by the ways and ask the wayfarers, and see which is the good way. Walk in it.' But they in their stubbornness answered, saying to him, 'We shall not go.' Again he said to them, 'I established over you watchmen, that you might listen for the sound of the trumpet.' But they said to him again, 'We shall not hearken.' And this openly, publicly did they do in the days of Jeremiah when he preached to them the word of the Lord, and they answered him, saying, 'To the word which you have spoken to us in the name of the Lord we shall not hearken. But we shall do our own will and every word which goes out of our mouths, to offer up incense-offerings to other gods' (Jer. 44:16–17)." That is why God turned to the peoples: "When he saw that they would not listen to him, he turned to the peoples, saying to them, 'Hear O peoples, and know, O church which is among them, and hearken, O land, in its fullness' (Jer. 6:18–19)." So who is now Israel? It is the peoples, no longer the old Israel: "By the name of Jacob [now] are called the people which is of the peoples." That is the key to Aphrahat's case. The people that was a no people, that people that had assembled out of the people, has now replaced Israel.

Like Eusebius, Aphrahat maintained that the peoples had been called to God before the people of Israel: "See, my beloved, that the vocation of the peoples was recorded before the vocation of the people. But because the time of the peoples had not come, and another was [to be] their redeemer, Moses was not persuaded that a redeemer and a teacher would come for the people which was of the peoples, which was greater and more worthy than the people of Israel." The people that was a no-people should not regard itself as alien to God: "If they should say, 'Us has he called alien children,' they have not been called alien children, but sons and heirs . . . But the peoples are those who hearken to God and were lamed and kept back from the ways of their sins." Indeed, the peoples produced believers who were superior in every respect to Israel: "Even from the old, whoever from among the peoples was pleasing to God was more greatly justified than Israel. Jethro the priest who was of the peoples and his seed were blessed: 'Enduring is his dwelling place, and his nest is set on a rock' (Num. 24:21)." Aphrahat here refers to the Gibeonites, Rahab, and various other Gentiles mentioned in the scriptural narrative.

Addressing his Christian hearers, Aphrahat then concludes, "By us they are provoked. On our account they do not worship idols, so that they will not be shamed by us, for we have abandoned idols and call lies the thing which our fathers left us. They are angry, their hearts are broken, for we have entered and have become heirs in their place. For theirs was this covenant which they had, not to worship other gods, but they did not accept it. By means of us he provoked them, and ours was the light and the life, as he preached, saying when he taught, 'I am the light of the world' (John 8:12)." So he concludes, "This brief memorial I have written to you concerning the peoples, because the Jews take pride and say, 'We are the people of God and the children of Abraham.' But we shall listen to John [the Baptist] who, when they took pride [saying], 'We are the children of Abraham,' then said to them, 'You should not boast and say, Abraham is father unto us, for from those very rocks can God raise up children for Abraham' (Matt. 3:9)."

So much for the challenge of those who held such views as

Aphrahat expresses. The case is complete: the people which is no-people, the people which is of the peoples, have taken the place of the people which claims to carry forward the salvific history of ancient Israel. The reason is in two complementary parts. First, Israel has rejected salvation and so lost its reason to exist; second, the no-people have accepted salvation and so gained its reason to exist. So the threads of the dispute link into a tight fabric: the shift in the character of politics, marked by the epochal triumph of Christianity in the state, bears profound meaning for the messianic mission of the church, and further, imparts a final judgment on the salvific claim of the competing nations of God: the church and Israel. What possible answer can sages have proposed to this indictment? Since at the heart of the matter lies the claim that Israel persists in the salvific heritage that has passed to the Christians, sages reaffirm that Israel persists—just as Paul had framed matters—after the flesh, an unconditional and permanent status. For one never ceases to be the son of his mother and his father, and the daughter is always the daughter of her father and her mother. So Israel after the flesh constitutes the family, in the most physical form, of Abraham, Isaac, and Jacob. Moreover, as that family, Israel inherits the heritage of salvation handed on by the patriarchs and matriarchs. The spiritualization of "Israel" here finds its opposite and counterpart: the utter and complete "genealogization" of Israel.

To the framers of Leviticus Rabbah, one point of emphasis proved critical: Israel remains Israel, the Jewish people, after the flesh, because Israel today continues the family begun by Abraham, Isaac, Jacob, Joseph and the other tribal founders, and bears the heritage bequeathed by them. That conviction of who is Israel never required articulation. The contrary possibility fell wholly outside of sages' (and all Jews') imagination. To state matters negatively, the people could no more conceive that they were not the daughters and sons of their fathers and mothers than that they were not one large family, that is, the family of Abraham, Isaac, and Jacob: Israel after the flesh. That is what "after the flesh" meant. The powerful stress on the enduring merit of the patriarchs and matriarchs, the social theory that treated Israel as one large, extended family, the actual children of Abraham, Isaac, and Jacob—these metaphors for the fleshly continuity surely met head-on the contrary position framed by Paul and restated by Christian theologians from his time onward. In this respect, while Aphrahat did not deny the "Israelness" of Israel, he did underline the futility of enduring as Israel. Maintaining that Israel would see no future salvation amounted to declaring that Israel, the Jewish people, pursued no worthwhile purpose in continuing to endure. Still, the argument is head-on and concrete: who is Israel? who enjoys salvation? To sages, as we shall see, the nations of the world serve God's purpose in ruling Israel, just as the prophets had said, and Israel, for its part, looks forward to a certain salvation.

The position of the framers of Leviticus Rabbah on the issues at hand emerges in both positive and negative formulation. On the positive side, Israel is God's first love. That position presents no surprises and can have been stated with equal relevance in any circumstances. We in no way can imagine that the authors of Leviticus Rabbah stress the points that they stress in particular because Christians have called them into question. I doubt that that was the case. In fact, when we survey the verses important to Aphrahat's case and ask what, in the counterpart writings of sages in all of late antiquity, people say about those same verses, we find remarkably little attention to the florilegium of proof texts adduced by Aphrahat.[6] While the argument on who is Israel did not take shape on the foundation of a shared program of verses, on which each party entered its position, the issue was one and the same. And the occasion—the political crisis of the fourth century—faced both parties.

Sages delivered a message particular to their system. The political context imparted to that message urgency for Israel beyond their small circle. As to confronting the other side, no sage would concede what to us is self-evident. This was the urgency of the issue. For the definition of what was at issue derived from the common argument of the age: who is the Messiah? Christ or someone else? Here, too, while the argument between Christian theologians and Judaic sages on the present status of Israel went forward on the same basic issues, it ran along parallel lines. True, lines of argument never intersected at all, just as in our review of sage's doctrine of the Messiah we could not find a point of intersection with the Christian position on the Christhood of

Jesus. The issue in both topics, however, is what was the same, even though the exposition of arguments on one side's proposition in no way intersected with the other side's.

When Aphrahat denied that God loves Israel any more, and contemporary sages affirmed that God yet loves Israel and always will, we come to a clearcut exchange of views on a common topic. Parallel to Aphrahat's sustained demonstrations on a given theme, the framers of Leviticus Rabbah laid forth thematic exercises, each one serving in a cumulative way to make a given point on a single theme. Therefore, in order to describe sages' position, we do well to follow their ideas in their own chosen medium of expression. I can find no more suitable way of recapitulating their reply to the question, Who is Israel? than by a brief survey of one of the sustained essays they present on the subject in Leviticus Rabbah. We proceed to the unfolding, in Leviticus Rabbah Parashah Two, of the theme: Israel is precious. At Lev. R. II:III.2.B, we find an invocation of the genealogical justification for the election of Israel: "He said to him, 'Ephraim, head of the tribe, head of the session, one who is beautiful and exalted above all of my sons will be called by your name: [Samuel, the son of Elkanah, the son of Jeroham,] the son of Tohu, the son of Zuph, an Ephraimite' [1 Sam. 1:1]; 'Jerobaom son of Nabat, an Ephraimite' [1 Sam. 11:26]. 'And David was an Ephraimite, of Bethlehem in Judah' (1 Sam. 17:12)." Since Ephraim, that is, Israel, had been exiled, the deeper message cannot escape our attention. Whatever happens, God loves Ephraim. However Israel suffers, God's love endures, and God cares. In context, that message brings powerful reassurance. Facing a Rome gone Christian, sages had to state the obvious, which no longer seemed self-evident at all. What follows spells out this very point: God is especially concerned with Israel.

II:IV

1. A. Returning to the matter (GWPH): "Speak to the children of Israel" (Lev. 1:2).

    B. R. Yudan in the name of R. Samuel b. R. Nehemiah: "The matter may be compared to the case of a king who had an undergarment, concerning which he instructed his servant, saying to him, 'Fold it, shake it out, and be careful about it!'

C. "He said to him, 'My lord, O king, among all the undergarments that you have, [why] do you give me such instructions only about this one?'

D. "He said to him, 'It is because this is the one that I keep closest to my body.'

E. "So too did Moses say before the Holy One, blessed be he, Lord of the Universe: 'Among the seventy distinct nations that you have in your world, [why] do you give me instructions only concerning Israel? [For instance,] "Command the children of Israel" [Num. 28:2], "Say to the children of Israel" [Ex. 33:5], "Speak to the children of Israel!" [Lev. 1:2].

F. "He said to him, 'The reason is that they stick close to me, in line with the following verse of Scripture: "For as the undergarment cleaves to the loins of a man, so have I caused to cleave unto me the whole house of Israel"'" (Jer. 13:11).

G. Said R. Abin, "[The matter may be compared] to a king who had a purple cloak, concerning which he instructed his servant, saying, 'Fold it, shake it out, and be careful about it!'

H. "He said to him, 'My Lord, O king, among all the purple cloaks that you have, [why] do you give me such instructions only about this one?'

I. "He said to him, 'That is the one that I wore on my coronation day.'

J. "So too did Moses say before the Holy One, blessed be he, Lord of the Universe: 'Among the seventy distinct nations that you have in your world, [why] do you give instructions to me only concerning Israel? [For instance,] "Say to the children of Israel," "Command the children of Israel," "Speak to the children of Israel."'

K. "He said to him, 'They are the ones who at the [Red] Sea declared me to be king, saying, "The Lord will be king"'" (Ex. 15:18).

The point of the passage has to do with Israel's particular

relationship to God: Israel cleaves to God, declares God to be king, and accepts God's dominion. Further evidence of God's love for Israel derives from the commandments themselves. God watches over every little thing that Jews do, even caring what they eat for breakfast. The familiar stress on the keeping of the laws of the Torah as a mark of hope finds fulfillment here: the laws testify to God's deep concern for Israel. So there is sound reason for high hope, expressed in particular in keeping the laws of the Torah. Making the matter explicit, Simeon b. Yohai (Lev. R. II:V.1.A–B) translates this fact into a sign of divine favor:

II:V

1. A. Said R. Simeon b. Yohai, "[The matter may be compared] to a king who had an only son. Every day he would give instructions to his steward, saying to him, 'Make sure my son eats, make sure my son drinks, make sure my son goes to school, make sure my son comes home from school.'

    B. "So every day the Holy One, blessed be he, gave instructions to Moses, saying, 'Command the children of Israel,' 'Say to the children of Israel,' 'Speak to the children of Israel.'"

We now come to the statement of how Israel wins and retains God's favor. The issue at hand concerns Israel's relationship to the nations before God, which is corollary to what has gone before. It is in two parts. First, Israel knows how to serve God in the right way. Second, the nations, though they do what Israel does, do things wrong. Israel does things right. Why then is Israel beloved? The following answers that question.

V:VIII

1. A. R. Simeon b. Yohai taught, "How masterful are the Israelites, for they know how to find favor with the creator."

    E. Said R. Hunia [in Aramaic:], "There is a tenant farmer who knows how to borrow things, and there is a tenant farmer who does not know how to borrow. The one who knows how to borrow combs his hair, brushes off his clothes, puts on a good face, and then goes over to the overseer of his work to borrow from him. [The overseer] says to him, 'How's the land doing?' He says to him, 'May you have the merit of being fully satisfied with its [wonderful] produce.' 'How are the oxen doing?' He says to him, 'May you have the merit of being fully satisfied with their fat.' 'How are the goats doing?' 'May you have the merit of being fully satisfied with their young.' 'And what would you like?' Then he says, 'Now if you might have an extra ten denars, would you give them to me?' The overseer replies, 'If you want, take twenty.'

F. "But the one who does not know how to borrow leaves his hair a mess, his clothes filthy, his face gloomy. He too goes over to the overseer to borrow from him. The overseer says to him, 'How's the land doing?' He replies, 'I hope it will produce at least what [in seed] we put into it.' 'How are the oxen doing?' 'They're scrawny.' 'How are the goats doing?' 'They're scrawny too.' 'And what do you want?' 'Now if you might have an extra ten denars, would you give them to me?' The overseer replies, 'Go, pay me back what you already owe me!'"

If Aphrahat had demanded a direct answer, he could not have received a more explicit one. He claims Israel does nothing right. Sages counter, speaking in their own setting of course, that they do everything right. Sages then turn the tables on the position of Aphrahat—again addressing it head-on. While the nations may do everything Israel does, they do it wrong.

Sages recognized in the world only one counterpart to Israel, and that was Rome. Rome's history formed the counterweight to Israel's. So Rome as a social entity weighed in the balance against Israel. That is why we return to the corollary question: who is Rome? For we can know who is Israel only if we can also explain who is Rome. Explaining who is Rome takes on urgency at the moment at which Rome presents to Israel problems of an unprecedented character. The matter belongs in any picture of who is Israel. Sages' doctrine of Rome forms the counterpart to Christian theologians' theory on who is Israel. Just as Aphrahat explains both who are the Christians and also who is Israel today, so sages in Leviticus Rabbah develop an important theory on who is Rome. They, too, propose to account for the way things are, and that means they have to explain who is this counterpart to Israel. And the sages' theory does respond directly to the question raised by the triumph of Christianity in the Roman Empire. For, as we shall see, the characterization of Rome in Leviticus Rabbah bears the burden of their judgment on the definition of the Christian people, as much as the sages' characterization of Rome in Leviticus Rabbah expressed their judgment of the place of Rome in the history of Israel.

To understand that position on the character of Rome, we have first of all to see that it constitutes a radical shift in the characterization of Rome in the unfolding canon of the sages' Judaism. For the treatment of Rome shifts in a remarkable way from the earlier approach to the subject. Rome in the prior writings, the Mishnah (ca. 200 C.E.) and the Tosefta (ca. 300–400 C.E.), stood for a particular place. We begin, once more, with the view of the Mishnah. For matters show a substantial shift in the characterization of Rome from the earlier to the later writings. Had matters remained pretty much the same from late second-century to fourth- and early fifth-century writings, we could not maintain that what is said in the fourth-century documents testifies in particular to intellectual events of the fourth century. We should have to hold that, overall, the doctrine was set and endured in its original version. What happened later on would then have no bearing upon the doctrine at hand, and my claim of a confrontation on a vivid issue would not find validation. But the doctrine of Rome does shift from the Mishnah to the fourth-century sages' writings: Leviticus Rabbah, Genesis Rabbah, and the Talmud of the Land of Israel. That fact proves the consequence, in the interpretation of ideas held in the fourth century, of the venue of documents in that time.

We have already seen the adumbration of the position that, in Leviticus Rabbah, would come to remarkably rich expression. Rome now stood for much more than merely a place among other places. Rome took up a place in the unfolding of the empires— Babylonia, Media, Greece, then Rome. Still more important, Rome is the penultimate empire on earth. Israel will constitute the ultimate one. That message, seeing the shifts in world history in a pattern and placing at the apex of the shift Israel itself, directly and precisely takes up the issue made urgent just now: the advent of the Christian emperors. Why do I maintain that in the characterization of Rome as the fourth and penultimate empire/animal sages address issues of their own day? Because Rome, among the successive empires, bears special traits, most of which derive from the distinctively Christian character of Rome.

Rome is represented as only Christian Rome can have been represented: it looks kosher but it is un-kosher. Pagan Rome cannot ever have looked kosher, but Christian Rome, with its appeal to ancient Israel, could and did and moreover claimed to. It bore some traits that validate, but lacked others that validate—just as Jerome said of Israel. It would be difficult to find a more direct confrontation between two parties to an argument. Now the issue is the same, Who is the true Israel? and the proof texts are the same; moreover, the prooftexts are read in precisely the same way. Only the conclusions differ!

The polemic represented in Leviticus Rabbah by the symbolization of Christian Rome makes the simple point that Christians are no different from and no better than pagans; they are essentially the same. The Christians' claim to form part of Israel, then, requires no serious attention. Since Christians came to Jews with precisely that claim, the sages' response—they are another Babylonia—bears a powerful polemic charge. But that is not the whole story, as we see. Second, just as Israel had survived Babylonia, Media, Greece, so would they endure to see the end of Rome (whether pagan, whether Christian). But there is a third point. Rome really does differ from the earlier, pagan empires, and that polemic shifts the entire discourse once we hear its symbolic vocabulary properly. For the new Rome really did differ from the old. Christianity was not merely part of a succession of undifferentiated modes of paganism. The symbols assigned to Rome attributed worse, more dangerous traits than those assigned to the earlier empires. The pig pretends to be clean, just as the Christians give the signs of adherence to the God of Abraham, Isaac, and Jacob. That much the passage concedes. For the pig is not clean, exhibiting some but not all of the required indications; and Rome is not Israel, even though it shares Israel's scripture. That position, denying to Rome in its Christian form a place in the family of Israel, forms the counterpart to the view of Aphrahat that Israel today is no longer Israel — again, a confrontation on issues. I present only the critical passage at which the animals that are invoked include one that places Rome at the interstices, partly kosher, partly not, therefore more dangerous than anyone else.

XII:V

9. A. Moses foresaw what the evil kingdoms would do [to Israel].

B. "The camel, rock badger, and hare" (Deut. 14:7). [Compare: "Nevertheless, among those that chew the cud or part the hoof, you shall not eat these: the camel, because it chews the cud but does not part the hoof, is unclean to you. The rock badger, because it chews the cud but does not part the hoof, is unclean to you. And the hare, because it chews the cud but does not part the hoof, is unclean to you, and the pig, because it parts the hoof and is cloven-footed, but does not chew the cud, is unclean to you" (Lev. 11:4–8).]

C. The camel (GML) refers to Babylonia, [in line with the following verse of scripture: "O daughter of Babylonia, you who are to be devastated!] Happy will be he who requites (GML) you, with what you have done to us" (Ps. 147:8).

D. "The rock badger" (Deut. 14:7) — this refers to Media.

E. Rabbis and R. Judah b. R. Simon.

F. Rabbis say, "Just as the rock badger exhibits traits of uncleanness and traits of cleanness, so the kingdom of Media produced both a righteous man and a wicked one."

G. Said R. Judah b. R. Simon, "The last Darius was Esther's son. He was clean on his mother's side and unclean on his father's side."

H. "The hare" (Deut. 14:7) — this refers to Greece. The mother of King Ptolemy was named "Hare" [in Greek: lagos].

I. "The pig" (Deut. 14:7) — this refers to Edom [Rome].

J. Moses made mention of the first three in a single verse

and the final one in a verse by itself [(Deut. 14:7, 8)]. Why so?

K. R. Yohanan and R. Simeon b. Laqish.

L. R. Yohanan said, "It is because [the pig] is equivalent to the other three."

M. And R. Simeon b. Laqish said, "It is because it outweighs them."

N. R. Yohanan objected to R. Simeon b. Laqish, "'Prophesy, therefore, son of man, clap your hands [and let the sword come down twice, yea thrice]' (Ezek. 21:14)."

O. And how does R. Simeon b. Laqish interpret the same passage? He notes that [the threefold sword] is doubled (Ezek. 21:14).

In the apocalypticizing of the animals of Lev. 11:4–8/Deut. 14:7 — the camel, rock badger, hare, and pig—the pig, standing for Rome, again emerges as different from the others and more threatening than the rest. Just as the pig pretends to be a clean beast by showing the cloven hoof, but in fact, is an unclean one, so Rome pretends to be just, but in fact, governs by thuggery. Edom does not pretend to praise God, but only blasphemes. It does not exalt the righteous, but kills them. These symbols concede nothing to Christian monotheism and veneration of the Torah of Moses (in its written medium). Of greatest importance, while all the other beasts bring further ones in their wake, the pig does not: "It does not bring another kingdom after it." It will restore the crown to the one who will truly deserve it, Israel. Esau will be judged by Zion, so Obad. 1:21.

Now how has the symbolization delivered an implicit message? It is in the treatment of Rome as distinct but essentially equivalent to the former kingdoms. This seems to me a stunning way of saying that the now-Christian empire in no way requires differentiation from its pagan predecessors. Nothing has changed, except matters have gotten worse. Beyond Rome, standing in a straight line with the others, lies the true shift in history, the rule of Israel and the cessation of the dominion of the (pagan) nations.

Leviticus Rabbah came to closure, it is generally agreed, around 400 C.E., that is, approximately a century after the Roman Empire in the east had begun to become Christian, and half a century after the last attempt to rebuild the Temple in Jerusalem had failed—a tumultuous age indeed. Accordingly, we have had the chance to see how distinctive and striking are the ways in which the symbols of animals that stand for the four successive empires of humanity and point towards the messianic time serve the framers' message. Rome in the fourth century became Christian. Sages responded by facing that fact quite squarely and saying, "Indeed, it is as you say, a kind of Israel, an heir of Abraham as your texts explicitly claim. But we remain the sole legitimate Israel, the bearer of the birthright—we and not you. So you are our brother: Esau, Ishmael, Edom." And the rest follows.

Sages framed their political ideas within the metaphor of genealogy, because to begin with, they appealed to the fleshly connection, the family, as the rationale for Israel's social existence. A family beginning with Abraham, Isaac, and Jacob, Israel today could best sort out its relationships by drawing into the family other social entities with which it found it had to relate. So Rome became the brother. That affinity came to light only when Rome had turned Christian, and that point marked the need for the extension of the genealogical net. But the conversion to Christianity also justified sages' extending membership in the family to Rome, for Christian Rome shared with Israel the common patrimony of scripture, and said so. The two facts, the one of the social and political metaphor by which sages interpreted events, the other of the very character of Christianity, account for the striking shift in the treatment of Rome that does appear to have taken place in the formative century represented by work on Leviticus Rabbah.

The Aftermath

Judaism endured in the West for two reasons. First, Christianity permitted it; second, Israel wanted it to. The fate of paganism in the fourth century shows the importance of the first of the two factors. We see, in particular, that it was not the intellectual power of sages alone that secured the long-term triumph of Judaism. It also was the character of the Christian emperors' policy toward Judaism that afforded to Jews and their religion such toleration as they would enjoy then and thereafter. The religious worship of

Judaism never was prohibited. Pagan sacrifice, by contrast, came under interdict in 341. Festivals went on into the fifth century, but the die was cast. When, after 350, Constantius won the throne over a contender who had enjoyed pagan support, he closed all the temples in the empire, prohibited access under penalty of death, and tolerated the storming and destruction of the temples. Churches took the place of pagan temples. That is not to suggest that paganism was extirpated overnight, or that all the laws were kept. It is an indication of an ongoing policy. The Christian emperors never instituted a parallel policy toward Judaism and the synagogue. The reason for the limited toleration accorded to Judaism need not detain us even though, as a political fact, it is the single most important reason for the continued survival of the Jews (therefore also of Judaism) in Western civilization.[7]

Pagan intellectuals, counterparts to the Judaic sages, responded with profound and systematic answers to Christian doctrine. No one familiar with their writing can suppose paganism lacked the power of ideas afforded to Israel by the Judaic sages. The contrary was the case. Iamblichus, a principal figure in the first half of the century, accomplished what Geffcken calls "the inner strengthening of paganism." This he did not by a negative statement on Christianity but a positive reassertion of pagan doctrine in a profoundly philosophical idiom, bearing deep overtones of religious feeling. Geffcken cites the following statement, "It is the fulfillment of ineffable rites the fitting accomplishment of which surpasses an intellectual understanding and the power of unspeakable signs which are intelligible to the gods alone that effect theurgic union." Iamblichus inspired Julian, and for a brief moment, it appeared that paganism would enjoy a renaissance. On intellectual grounds, it might have. But afterward a severe repression set in, and the Christian emperors Gratian, Valentinian II, and Theodosius undertook a systematic counterattack.

The laws came one after the other. In 381, pagans were denied the right to bequeath property; sacrifice was again prohibited; Gratian deprived the temples and cults of their property and subsidies. So the institutions of paganism lost their foundations. And that was a fact of state policy and politics to which doctrine, on the pagan side, hardly pertained. The upshot, as Geffcken says, was the end of pagan cult: "For without the substructure of religious observance within the framework of the state, there could be no pagan cult, no ancestral worship." True enough, Christian people, led by monks, implemented the laws' spirit through their own actions, destroying temples (as well as synagogues). For their part, pagan intellectuals at the end of the century, typified by Libanius, responded with a program of argument and rhetoric. But the issue was not to be resolved through rhetoric, nor was the fate of the temples settled by mobs. It was a political attack that paganism confronted, and with the throne in Christian hands, the policy of the church settled matters. Anti-pagan legislation won the day, to be sure not everywhere and all at once, but ultimately and completely. That fact proves what might have happened to Judaism. But it did not happen, as I said, in part because the church-state did not choose to extirpate Judaism. The other reason we locate in the intellectual achievements of the Judaic sages.

These require only a rapid reprise. With the triumph of Christianity through Constantine and his successors in the West, Christianity's explicit claims, now validated in world-shaking events of the age, demanded a reply. The sages of the Talmud of the Land of Israel, Genesis Rabbah and Leviticus Rabbah, provided it. At those very specific points at which the Christian challenge met head-on Israel's world view, sages' doctrines responded.

What did Israel's sages have to present as the Torah's answer to the cross? It was the Torah and its doctrine of history, Messiah, and Israel. History in the beginning, in Genesis, accounted for the events of the day. The Messiah will be a sage of the Torah. Israel today comprises the family, after the flesh, of the founders of Israel. The Torah therefore served as the encompassing symbol of Israel's salvation. The Torah would be embodied in the person of the Messiah who, of course, would be a rabbi. The Torah confronted the cross, with its doctrine of the triumphant Christ, Messiah and king, ruler now of earth as of heaven. In the formulation of the sages who wrote the fourth- and early fifth-century documents (the Talmud of the Land of Israel and Genesis and Leviticus Rabbah), the Torah thus confronted the challenge of the cross of Christianity as, later on, with its ample doctrines of history, Messiah, and Israel, it would meet and (in Israel, in particular) overcome the sword and crescent of Islam. Within Israel, the Torah everywhere triumphed. That is why, when Christianity came to power and commenced to define the civilization of the West, Judaism met and overcame its greatest crisis before modern times. And it held. As a result, Jews remained within the Judaic system of the dual Torah. That is why they continued for the entire history of the West to see the world through the worldview of the dual Torah and to conduct life in accord with the way of life of the Torah as the rabbis explained it. The Judaism of the dual Torah took shape in response to the crisis of Constantine's conversion and came to its systematic literary expression in the writings of the following century, from the Talmud of the Land of Israel (ca. 400) through Genesis Rabbah, Leviticus Rabbah, Pesiqta deRav Kahana, The Fathers According to Rabbi Nathan, and beyond. That Judaism took up the ineluctable and urgent question of salvation as Christianity framed that question. And, for believing Israel, the answer proved self-evidently true, then and for long centuries afterward.

The consequence was stunning success for that society for which, in sages' view, God cared so deeply: eternal Israel after the flesh. For Judaism in the rabbis' statement did endure in the Christian West, imparting to Israel the secure conviction of constituting that Israel after the flesh to which the Torah continued to speak. How do we know sages' Judaism won? Because when, in turn, Islam gained its victory, Christianity throughout the Middle East and North Africa gave way. Christianity endured, to be sure, but not as the religion of the majorities of the Roman Middle East and North Africa, areas that for many centuries prior to Islam had formed the heartland of Christianity. Chalcedonian and non-Chalcedonian Christian churches continued under Islamic rule and endure even today. But the Islamic character of the Near and Middle East and North Africa tells the story of what really happened, which was a debacle for Christianity. But sages' Judaism in those same vast territories retained the loyalty and conviction of the people of the Torah. The cross would rule only where the crescent and its sword did not. But the Torah of Sinai everywhere and always sanctified Israel in time and promised secure salvation for eternity. So Israel believed and so does faithful

Israel, those Jews who also are Judaists, believe today. The entire history of Judaism is contained within these simple propositions.

The political circumstances of the fourth century—ascendant Christianity, a still political Judaism—hardly could remain stable. By the turn of the fifth century the state was firmly Christian and its successors in Europe would remain so for fifteen hundred years. The sages' framing of a Judaic system attained the status of the norm. So far as Christianity in all of its European forms raised challenges to Judaism in its one, now normative form, answers found in the fourth century retained for Jews the standing of self-evident truth. We therefore should anticipate no rehearsal of that odd moment at which, each in his own idiom, a Judaic sage and a Christian theologian could address the same issue and compose a position based on the same facts and modes of argument. When, under the conditions that prevailed eight hundred to a thousand years later, new encounters took place, they bore no resemblance in intellectual structure to the one we have reviewed. Then, as before the fourth century, different people talked about different things to different people—even when they met face to face.

Why the initial confrontation produced no later continuation finds its answer in an essentially political circumstance. Conditions for debate later on did not accord equal standing to both sides, such as the Judaic sages of the fourth century assuredly enjoyed and the Christian theologians accorded, as best they could. What this meant, curiously, was that the confrontation later on took place jointly—not by indirection, through sustained writings on a given theological issue treated wholly in its own terms—and through direct interlocution of one side by the other. In that respect, too, the later, and enduring confrontation did not replicate the mode of discourse of the initial phase, which was marked by the composition of large-scale writings clear of all marks of an argument such as I have composed: same issues, same facts, same mode of thought.

We do not have to imagine what one side would have said to the other. We know what each did say to the other. In no way can we characterize the discourse as an interesting argument about issues important to each side, defined in the same way by each party to the discussion. Quite to the contrary, the issues facing the Judaic participants bore a political, not an intellectual character.

The rights of Jews to live where and how they did were at stake in the disputations; the beliefs of the Jews about the meaning and end of history, the Messiah in the end of days, and the definition of Israel scarcely came up. When they did, Christians framed the issue, and Jews responded to the Christian framing of the issue: Why do you *not* believe? Nor, in their response, did the Jewish participants vastly improve on matters. They simply ridiculed the Christians' convictions: "they lacked both *ratio* and *auctoritas*," being devoid of scriptural foundation and without logical justification. So Peter Berger. No debate occurred there, scarcely an intellectual confrontation.[8]

The next major intellectual confrontation on the side of Judaism took place eight hundred years later in the twelfth century. Then the Christian side took the offensive, and in Berger's judgment, "We find Jews arguing that Christianity is so inherently implausible that only the clearest biblical evidence could suffice to establish its validity." Issues of the initial confrontation scarcely occur in the medieval debates between Judaic and Christian officials, at least, not in their classical formulation. An account of the disputations of the Middle Ages—Paris, 1240; Barcelona, 1263; and Tortosa, 1413-1414—therefore carries us into a world far removed from the one in which the issues of history, Messiah, and Israel produced a genuine confrontation on the same set of issues, defined in the same terms.[9]

Of special interest here is the bearing these later debates have on the thesis at hand. Specifically, can we identify a political foundation that made common discourse necessary, even urgent? Can we find points of public policy, not merely theological doctrine, that debate was meant to settle? The answer is one-sidedly affirmative. So Maccoby: "The authority of the Inquisition did extend to some regulation of Judaism." The presence of kings and high lords temporal as well as lords spiritual who bore considerable responsibility in public administration leaves no doubt on that score. Yet in other ways I see no important continuity at all. When Judaic sages and Christian theologians constructed what I take to have been an argument, they addressed issues of mutual interest. The argument was joined fairly on matters of theological substance, each side working out its position free of the intervention of the other. But in the medieval disputations, Judaism stood at the dock, the accused. The charge for Paris, in 1240 was that Judaism in the Talmud taught blasphemies against the Christian religion, made remarks against Christians, revered holy books that contained unedifying material, e.g., nonsense or obscenity.

The issues at Barcelona, 1263, prove somewhat more interesting. Maccoby sees it as a debate rather than an inquisition. The Christian approach now was "to attempt to prove the truth of Christianity from the Jewish writings, including the Talmud." So Maccoby:

> Various Aggadic passages, collected from Talmud and Midrash, were thought to support Christian doctrines, especially the divinity of the Messiah, his suffering on the cross, the date of his advent, and his promulgation of a new law. Nahmanides immediately challenged the rationale of this contention.

In consequence of this approach, a further issue derived from the authority of the so-called Aggadic portions of the Talmud. The Judaic side treated the passages as unimportant, though the rabbis of the day revered them. Maccoby's judgment that there was a basic "lack of rapprochement and mutual understanding in the disputations" proves definitive: no argument here, only a confrontation lacking all shared discourse.[10]

As to Tortosa, 1413-1414, chaired by a pope and joined by representatives of the Jewish communities of Aragon and Catalonia, the disputation aimed at the conversion of the Jews.[11] Maccoby's judgment is this: "As far as the larger issues of Jewish-Christian confrontation were concerned, it added little to the Barcelona Disputation." But one thing is clear from Maccoby's fine summary: a matter of public policy greatly engaged the Judaic side, specifically, religious toleration. As one of the Jewish spokesmen stated:

> I say that all disputation about a principle of religion is prohibited, so that a man may not depart from the principles of his religion. It seems that only science should be made the subject of dispute and argument, but religion and belief ought

to be consigned willingly to faith, not argument, so that he may not retreat from it.

Europe would have to endure the devastation, in the name of religion, of Germany and much else before even that much toleration might win support as a political policy, then in the form of *cuius regio eius religio*—not much toleration, but better than nothing. In any event the focus of discourse was this: "to prove the truth of Christian doctrines about the Messiah from certain passages in the Talmud." Judaic sages cannot have found very urgent the needs of such an agenda.[12]

I see no point of contact between the shape of the initial confrontation and the intellectual program, such as it was, of the medieval continuation. In fact, the two programs for debate seem to me—in selection and definition of the issues, in the manner of argument, and in the kinds of proofs people adduced in evidence of their propositions—wholly different from one another. In form and substance, context and content, the initial confrontation generated no succession. In the fourth century two political entities confronted one another out of rough parity, meeting for a brief moment as the one ascended, the other declined. In the medieval confrontations political parity hardly characterized both parties to the dispute, which yielded confrontation but no debate, and all the more so, no dialogue.

In the fourth century, Christian theologians could consider in essentially the same terms as Judaic sages the scriptural issues they (correctly) deemed critical for Judaism. Aphrahat, of course, forms the exemplary figure, arguing so carefully on the basis of ancient Israelite writings when addressing contemporary Jews. But I do not see the others as much different from Aphrahat. Eusebius addressed issues of world-historical interpretation, doing so in a rational and civil manner. Jerome wanted to engage in serious, equal argument with Jews, and so he took most seriously the lessons they had to teach—again, an encounter between equals. Chrysostom alas! But he did not argue as an equal to Judaic competition, rather as a beleaguered and harassed figure, fearful of the future of Christians new to the church and impressed by the synagogue. Eusebius, Chrysostom, Aphrahat, each in his way, addressed the other side by indirection, each with dignity, each in defense of the new faith. Later on, when the encounter became a confrontation that was direct and provocative, it turned into a confrontation not between equals, not conducted with much dignity, and not aimed at clarifying for the faith within the issues of the challenge from the counterpart without. And this shift in tone and in substance, in the symbolic expression of the issues, expresses a more profound shift in the political realitites which dictated and defined the terms of the tragic confrontation of the Middle Ages. In the fourth century, sages of Judaism could pretend to ignore the challenge of Christianity, while at the same time systematically countering that challenge. Christian theologians forthrightly could enter the encounter with Judaism as with an equal. In the twelfth, thirteenth, and fourteenth centuries circumstances in no way afforded such an encounter.

The relevance to our own day demands only passing attention. Today Christianity controls few governments but much moral authority, exercises little power to dictate public policy, though (in my view, quite properly) much power of public persuasion. Not hiding in the catacombs, but also not determining the shape of the West, Christianity enjoys a position in the world of politics more like what it had in the time of Constantine—influential, but not (yet) in charge—than in the age of the medieval disputations. And for its part, Judaism, in the persons of Israel after the flesh, in the West (not to mention in the State of Israel!) enjoys the protection of law that in medieval times proved not entirely reliable. So argument between people equal at both a political and an intellectual level may now go forward once more. Consequently, on account of the character of the politics of the contemporary West, for both sides, civil equality exists. Civil discourse with subtlety, by indirection, and through learning once more regains the platform. People can now, again, agree on issues, negotiate modes of common argument, concur on the facts that will be probative—that is to say, write books for one another to read.

5

The Absoluteness of Christianity and the Uniqueness of Judaism

Why Salvation is not of the Jews

The publication more than a half-century ago of Billerbeck's convenient compendium of ready references in the rabbinic literature to New Testament topics only accelerated the trend, well under way from the end of the nineteenth century, to appeal to rabbinic writings for solutions of intractable problems in New Testament exegesis. These concerned particularly arcane matters in the writings of Paul and in the Gospels, for instance, the law in Paul, the doctrine of the Messiah and salvation in the Gospels. Indeed, it was said that if a saying could be shown to be "Jewish" and not "Greek," then Jesus really said it. Stated with more probity, the position was simple. People expected to find in the writings of Judaism pretty much the way things were, and that would permit them to make sense of what Paul and the evangelists had to say. They wished to read the letters and stories as arguments with opponents accurately represented as to their opinions, outsiders who stood for other positions, framed in their own terms, subject to criticism and rejection by the nascent faith. Christianity then came to be represented as a kind of reform of Judaism, not as an absolute and autonomous religion on its own.

Not only so, but the incipient movement in the rapprochement of Judaism and Christianity in the twentieth century, made urgent by the catastrophe of World War II, added impetus to the movement. Consequently, debates on the covenantal nature of "the law" or on the conception of law in "Judaism" flourish not in rabbinical but in Christian theological circles. The contemporary impasse in Pauline studies draws attention to arcane matters of concern not to Paul and those who preserved and canonized his writings, but to those whose reading of the Old Testament covenant Paul tells us that he rejected. By now it has become increasingly evident that to understand Paul's view of "Judaism," we have to understand (only) Paul—there being no Judaism "out there"[1]—attested by sources outside of the Pauline corpus that appeal to classifications and categories common to those of Paul and so available for comparison with Paul's picture. And that leads us to a theological judgment with implications for the interpretation of both Christian and Judaic writings of late antiquity.

It is the simple point that Christianity is absolute and Judaism is unique (to use the correct language of their respective theologies). In fact, there can be no dialogue between an entity that is sui generis and any other entity, and given the correct insistence of Christianity on its absoluteness and of Judaism on its uniqueness, genuine dialogue falls beyond the limits of logical discourse. The implications for New Testament hermeneutics will prove self-evident. The blurring of the boundaries between the one and the other, the representation of Christianity as a kind of Judaism, the appeal to Judaism for validation and judgment of Christianity—these familiar traits of contemporary biblical and theological studies obscure that simple fact.

Christianity began on the first Easter. It is, therefore, absolute in its reading of its circumstance and context. It is not a kind of Judaism. It is wholly other. The absolute standing of Christianity finds expression in its view that in all time and in eternity, there has been and there can be only one, unique, absolute incarnation, that of Jesus Christ raised from the dead, and only one gospel, the gospel of the salvation of Jesus Christ.

The Judaic writings that have become normative as the Judaism of the dual Torah lay claim, by no means alone among Judaisms, to the counterpart position, namely, the uniqueness of "Israel," meaning the Jewish people after the flesh. There is only that one people in the genus which it defines; all other peoples are a different genus of people altogether. The experience of Jewry forms a history that is continuous, however disjointed, and that also takes place out of phase with all other peoples' histories. Genesis Rabbah, one of the monuments of rabbinic biblical exegesis, represents "Israel" as the counterpart to Adam, and Israel's history as the counterpart to the story of Eden. Adam's fall led to the ultimate degradation of humanity; the restoration began with Abraham and reached its conclusion at Sinai with Moses and Israel. To Christian theologians the picture is a familiar one, with Jesus Christ, the last Adam, serving as "Israel" does in the theology of Judaism as the centerpiece of the claim of absoluteness (Christian) or uniqueness (Judaic). And we know that in the history and comparison of religion, the component of a religious system that a religion identifies as unique and therefore beyond all sharing or communication with outsiders, brings us to the center of matters.

In that context, the premise that the holy books of Christianity are to be read in light of Judaic counterparts forms an odd and jarring conviction. To revert to the example of Paul, when people appeal to Judaic writings of any setting and of any period of composition, even long after the first century, to explain what Paul meant by the law, they violate not only rules of historical relevance. They also disrupt the natural flow of theological thinking. The reason is that they assume a continuity where there has been, and can only have been, a radical break; they bridge an abyss beyond all reckoning. Let me make the point with heavy emphasis: *The upshot is to assume that people can have understood one another, who in point of fact, have no language in common.*

Before proceeding let me introduce an important distinction in the analysis of the relationships between religious systems. It is between a fact that is systemically vital and one that is inert. For the study of economics, this point has been made by Joseph A. Schumpeter as follows: "In economics as elsewhere, most statements of fundamental facts acquire importance only by the superstructures they are made to bear and are commonplace in the absence of such superstructures."[2] That is to say, a system of religious thought, comprising a world view, a way of life, and a definition of the social entity meant to adopt the one and embody the other, makes ample use of available facts. In order to make their statement, the authors of the documents of such a system speak in a language common to their age. Some of these facts form part of the background of discourse, like the laws of gravity. They are, if important, in no way central, because they bear no portion of the burden of the systemic message. I call such facts inert. Other of these facts form centerpieces of the system; they may or may not derive from the common background. Their importance to the system forms part of the statement and testimony of that system. The fact that the legal requirements of the Jews of Palestine ("Israel" in the "Land of Israel") of the first century insisted upon a writ of divorce when a marriage came to an end is critical in understanding debates on correct grounds for divorce. But it is an inert, not a systemically active fact. We have to know that fact, but when we do, we still have not properly entered into the systemic importance (if any) of sayings on acceptable grounds for divorce.

Let me give one unimportant example of the difference between an inert and a systemically vital fact, drawn from my own research,[3] though whole encyclopedias of New Testament exegesis exemplify the same fact. To understand the saying, "First cleanse the inside" (Luke 11:39, Matt. 23:25-26), we have to know that in someone's purity rules of the time in which the saying took shape, people treated as different domains, as to cultic unclean-ness, the inside of a goblet and the outside of the same goblet. Without knowing that fact, the saying is gibberish. But knowing that fact does not help us understand what Jesus (really) said or even meant. That fact is inert, forming the background for the statement that the saying wishes to make. The sense of the statement and its message derive from the theological context of the evangelists, which for Luke, addresses a different issue ("Give for alms those things which are within") from that critical to Matthew, whose Gospel aims at underlining the critique of scribes and Pharisees as hypocrites ("First cleanse the inside . . . that the outside also may be clean"). The inert fact contains valuable information for the study of Judaism in the period of the Gospels. As a matter of fact, for I have shown elsewhere, the Gospels' sayings presuppose a legal situation that differs from the rule that forms the premise for the rabbinic text in which the rule appears. The upshot is that we cannot understand the "First cleanse the inside" sayings without knowing "Judaism." But when we do know "Judaism," we still do not understand those sayings. For the use of the fact of "Judaism" testifies to the systemic intent and makes the system's statement, but that statement has no bearing whatever on the fact that is used. That is, then, an inert fact: interesting, but not very consequential. The case at hand therefore forms ample evidence for the importance, for understanding Judaism, of the Christian "background" (*Umwelt*), as much as understanding Christianity requires knowledge of the Jewish or Judaic "background." But in the nature of things, the same evidence testifies to the unimportance of knowing about Judaism for interpreting the Gospels and of knowing about Christianity for interpreting the law.

For neither is effectively the background for the other. When we come to systemically critical facts, there is no continuity let alone confrontation, and not even a connection. The criterion for connection surely derives from comprehension. For continuities to be established, such that interpreting a systemic detail in one system permits us to make sense of a systemic detail of another system entirely, we require some kind of dialogue, at least a confrontation. But what if we notice that one group simply cannot make sense of the message of the other? Then we have to call into question our premise that the system of the one presupposes not only facts, but the systemic statement, fully comprehended, of the other. People maintain that we cannot understand Christianity (in any form) if we do not understand Judaism (in all forms, e.g., Essene and Philonic and Rabbinic and what have you). They take as an article of academic conviction that Christianity was born out of Judaism, and they present as a foundation of contemporary interreligious dialogue that Christianity forms the daughter religion of Judaism.[4] But I shall now show, first through a case, then through general observations, that Judaism (in the system that became normative) and Christianity (in Gospels that became canonical) represent different people talking about different things to different people, with no possibility of mutual comprehension, let alone dialogue.

My particular case of the impossibility of mutual comprehension derives from Mark 11:15-19, the driving of the money-changers out of the Temple. With commendable confidence, some exegetes maintain that the sense and meaning of Jesus's action

will have been immediately comprehensible and self-evident.
Jesus will have been understood to have attacked the Temple. I
shall try to show the opposite: Jesus will not have been understood
at all, hence will have been regarded as a mere madman. It is
correctly alleged[5] that the money-changers performed an essential
service: "The money-changers were probably those who changed
the money in the possession of pilgrims into the coinage acceptable
by the Temple in payment of the half-shekel tax levied on all
Jews."[6] They charged a fee for doing so. In order to purchase
animals for sacrifice, pilgrims had to pay the appropriate fee, and
the money-change made it possible. Again Sanders: "The business
arrangements around the Temple were necessary if the commandments were to be obeyed." Interpreting this action of Jesus,
Sanders says that it symbolized destruction: "That is one of the
most obvious meanings of the action of overturning itself."[7]
Sanders states his interpretation in this way:

> Thus we conclude that Jesus publicly predicted or threatened
> the destruction of the Temple, that the statement was shaped
> by his expectation of the arrival of the eschaton, that he probably
> also expected a new Temple to be given by God from heaven,
> and that he made a demonstration which prophetically symbol-
> ized the coming event.[8]

Sander's interpretation is not at issue. What I wonder is whether,
to Jews familiar with scripture and the understanding of scripture
embodied in the Temple, the action will have had any obvious
meaning at all. To find out, we turn to a later document, for
reasons that will become clear presently. If we ask the authorship
of the Mishnah, ca. 200 C.E., to tell us why the money-changers
were in the Temple, they would give us a simple answer:

A. On the fifteenth of that same month [Adar, before Nisan]
   they set up money-changers' tables in the provinces.
B. On the twenty-fifth of Adar they set them up in the Temple.
C. Once they were set up in the Temple, they began to exact
   pledges from those who had not paid the tax in specie.
D. From whom do they exact a pledge?
E. Levites, Israelites, proselytes, and freed slaves, but not from
   women, slaves, and minors . . .

M. Sheqalim 1:3

Money-changers serve to change diverse coinage into the sheqel required for the Temple tax. They would take a pledge from one who has not yet paid his tax, and in exchange, supply the required half-sheqel. Money-changers were essentially for the collection of the tax. Why? I state with emphasis: *Because that tax, paid by all eligible Israelites, served through the coming year to provide the public daily whole offerings in the name of the community.* Those who did not have to pay the tax could do so, e.g., women, slaves, or minors, but a Gentile or a Samaritan could not pay the tax. They could contribute freewill offerings, but they could not participate in supplying the Temple tax of a half-sheqel. Thus far I go over the familiar consensus, as accurately portrayed by Sanders.

What is at stake in the changing of money is a very considerable consideration which pertains only to Israelite males as obligatory, other Israelites as voluntary. And what was that? To understand the place of the money-changers in the Temple, we require an answer to that question. It is supplied by the authorship of the Tosefta, an amplification of the Mishnah brought to closure about ca. 300 C.E. a century after the closure of the Mishnah.[9]

A. *Once they were set up in the Temple, they began to exact pledges from those who had not yet paid [M. Sheqalim 1:3c].*

B. They exact pledges from Israelites for their sheqels, so that the public offerings might be made [paid for] by using their funds.

C. This is like a man who got a sore on his foot, and the doctor had to force it and cut off his flesh so as to heal him. Thus did the Holy One, blessed be he, exact a pledge from Israelites for the payment of their sheqels, so that the public offerings might be made out of their funds.

D. For public offerings appease and effect atonement between Israel and their father in heaven.

E. Likewise we find of the heave offering of sheqels which the Israelites paid in the wilderness, as it is said, "And you shall take the atonement money from the people of Israel and shall appoint it for the service of the tent of meeting, that it may bring the people of Israel to remembrance before the Lord, so as to make atonement for yourselves" (Exod. 30:16)

Tosefta Sheqalim 1:6[10]

The proof text, Exod. 30:16, explicitly links the sheqel offering in the wilderness to the sheqel tax or offering in the Temple. Both attained atonement for sin. Not only so, but the parable, C, makes the matter explicit. The doctor has to cut off the flesh so as to heal the patient. The sin is the sore on the foot. The doctor has to force the sore and cut it off. The Holy One has to exact the pledge of the half-sheqel so as to make all Israelites responsible for the daily whole offerings, which atone for Israel's sin. The explanation for the payment of the sheqel tax forms a chapter in the larger conception of the daily whole offerings, a chapter commenced by the Exod. 30:16 explicit statement that the daily whole offering atones for the sin of each Israelite and all Israel every day. These daily whole offerings, it is clear, derive from communal funds, provided by every Israelite equally. They serve all Israelites, individually and collectively, as atonement for sin.

For the accomplishment of that holy purpose, the money-changers, as a matter of fact, were simply essential. They formed an integral part in the system of atonement and expiation for sin.[11] The explicit explanation of the payment of the half-sheqel, therefore, is that it allowed all Israelites to participate in the provision of the daily whole offering, which accomplished atonement for sin in behalf of the holy people as a whole. That explains why Gentiles and Samaritans may not pay the sheqel, while women, slaves, or minor Israelites may do so (M. Sheqalim 1:5A-B). Gentiles and Samaritans do not form part of "Israel," and therefore are unaffected by the expiation accomplished by the daily whole offering.

Now to the point at hand. Some maintain that everyone will have understood the meaning of Jesus's action. But I think the contrary is the fact. Anyone who understood that conception of the daily whole offering will have found incomprehensible and unintelligible an action of overturning the tables of the money-changers. Such an action will have provoked astonishment, since it will have called into question the very simple fact that the daily whole offering effected atonement and brought about expiation for sin, and God had so instructed Moses in the Torah. Accordingly, only someone who rejected the Torah's explicit teaching concerning the daily whole offering could have overturned the tables—or, as I shall suggest, someone who had in mind setting up a different table, and for a different purpose: for the action carries the entire message, both negative and positive. Indeed, the money-changers' presence made possible the cultic partici- pation of every Israelite, and it was not only not a blemish on the cult but part of its perfection. That is why I doubt that anyone could have understood what Jesus did, except, of course, for Jesus and his disciples. The gesture was in context simply beyond all comprehension.

We have to work our way back from the purpose of the daily whole offering to the task of the money-changers in order to understand the statement made by Jesus through his action. And it follows that no Jew of the time who deemed the Temple the place where Israel atoned for sin could have understood the meaning of Jesus' action, because nearly all Jews both in the Land of Israel and in the Exile took for granted that the daily whole- offerings expiated sin and so restored the relationship between God and Israel that sin spoiled. But I have also to add that everyone who grasped the context of Jesus' action will have appreciated the statement made by his action. That context was the establishment of the Eucharist, the rite of atonement and expiation of sin that Jesus would found within that same passion narrative to which the action before us formed a prologue—but also a counterpart.

The overturning of the money-changers' tables, as we have seen, represents an act of the rejection of the most important rite of the Israelite cult, the daily whole offering, and therefore, a statement that there is a means of atonement other than the daily whole offering, which is null. What, then, was to take the place of the daily whole offering? It was to be the rite of the Eucharist: table for table, whole offering for whole offering. It therefore seems to me that the correct context in which to read the overturning of the money-changers' tables is not the destruction of the Temple in general, but the institution of the sacrifice of the Eucharist, in particular. It further follows that the counterpart of Jesus' negative action in overturning one table must be his affirmative action in establishing or setting up another table, that is to say, I turn to the passion narratives centered upon the Last Supper. That, at any rate, is how, as an outsider to scholarship in this field, I should suggest we read the statement. The negative is that the atonement for sin achieved by the daily whole offering is null, and the positive, that atonement for sin is achieved by the Eucharist: one table overturned, another table set up in place, and both for the same purpose of atonement and expiation of sin. When we realize how the central actions in Jesus' life, as contemporary scholarship identifies them—first, the driving out of the money-changers; second, the institution of the Eucharist—correspond with one another, and when we recall how broadly the understanding of the daily whole offering will have circulated among Jews in general, we realize the utter incomprehensibility of Christianity in its initial stages and statement in the context of Judaism. The two religious traditions, Christianity and Judaism, in their first statements, really do represent people of one sort talking about different things to people of a different sort altogether.

This simple case may now lead to a broader generalization. I maintain that each group talked to its adherents about its points of urgent concern, that is, different people talking about different things to different people.[12] Incomprehension marks relations between Judaism and Christianity in the first century, even though the groups were two sectors of the same people. The reason is that each addressed its own agenda, spoke to its own issues, and employed language distinctive to its adherents. Neither exhibited understanding of what was important to the other.

When, for example, Jesus asked people who they thought he was, the enigmatic answer proved less interesting than the question posed. For the task he set himself, as portrayed by not only the Gospels but also Paul and the other New Testament writers, was to reframe everything people knew through encounter with what they did not know: a taxonomic enterprise. When the rabbis of late antiquity rewrote in their own image and likeness the entire scripture and history of Israel, dropping whole eras as though they had never been, ignoring vast bodies of old Jewish writing, inventing whole new books for the canon of Judaism, they did the same thing. They reworked what they had received in light of what they proposed to give.

What, then, has proved to define the stakes in the insistence that to understand Christian scriptures we need not merely inert facts but systemic statements that we identify as Judaic? As I see it, the urgency attached to that proposition derives from a positive and a negative motivation. The positive is the nurture of good will on the part of the majority-religion toward the small and hated minority-religion. That accounts for the whole of the Jews' interest and a considerable part of the Christians' in the appeal to Judaism for the solution of New Testament interpretive problems. But the other component of what is at stake has also to be recognized. It is wholly characteristic of Christian interest in the Judaic sources of Christianity. Since, as everyone knows, some earliest Christians were Jews and saw "the way" or their religion (i.e., what we would call "their Judaism") as normative and authoritative, a natural question troubling believing Christians arises: Why does Judaism as a whole remain a religion that believes other things about other subjects altogether?

Often asked negatively, the question turns on why the Jews do not believe, rather than on what they do believe. The upshot is that there really is no interest at all in "Judaism" in any form. In this respect contemporary ecumenical dialogue on the Christian part goes forward along the same lines, and for precisely the same reason that the earlier Christians, no longer "the old Israel" in their own estimation, took an interest in that "Judaism" that they claimed to confront. It is simply part of the systemic statement of Christianity to address Judaism with the question: Why not? That is to say, part of the existential requirement of being a Christian was to ask outsiders, beginning with Jews, Why not? For the asking of the question, Why not? rather than, Why so? reflects the long-term difficulty that the one group has had in making sense of the other—any other, that is, any outsider.[13] Responding by appeal to the nature and condition of Judaism has yielded those invidious comparisons, for instance, between legalistic Judaism and moral Christianity, that Christians of good will these days ordinarily set aside.[14] But the reading of the portrait of Judaism composed by Christianity, absolute and utterly different from all else, as an account of how things were, that is, as a picture of a Judaic system, remains as a legacy. We now understand that in the literature called *adversus judaeos*, Justin's Trypho, Aphrahat's "sage" or "debater of the people," and the like, form Christian inventions for the purposes of disputation. That invented, essentially fictive Judaism tells us only about the system builders who invented it, that is, the Christianity of the Christian *adversus judaeos* writers. It is not a Judaism that characterized any Judaic group, e.g., a set of system builders, whom we can now identify, or whose writings we can now adduce in evidence. That is why, I should suggest, in the interpretation of the New Testament and the formative centuries of Christianity, salvation is really not of the Jews, not at all.

6

Shalom

Complementarity

The conception of "shalom," as we all know, involves peace in the sense not merely of the absence of war, but the presence of a whole and complete state of complementarity.[1] Peace is peace when both parties affirm peace, meaning, when each party affirms the other. That commonplace comes to mind here and now in particular, because of the poignant confrontation that has taken place between two communities that prize peace and seek harmony, the Roman Catholic order of the Carmelites, and the community of Judaism formed by the survivors of the Holocaust. In the conflict presently working itself out in the matter of the location of a place of prayer and communion, we witness yet further evidence that peace is possible only when a whole and complementary understanding among different religions is attained. There can be no peace, nor even a truce, so long as one side within the framework of its religious convictions can make no sense of the other side within the framework of its religious conviction. And it is clear, the heart-breaking conflict that presently disfigures the peaceful and cooperative relationships between Judaism and Roman Catholic Christianity, nurtured by so many in all parts of the world, comes about because we do not know how to grasp the other, how to make sense of that other in our own framework and in our own terms.

Accordingly, at this very moment we confront an example of the future task of all religious intellectuals, which is to try to think through a religious theory of the other, a theory framed by each religion within its own terms but suitable for guiding the insider on how to think about the outsider. The single most important problem facing religion for the next hundred years, as for the last, is that single intellectual challenge: how to think through difference, how to account within one's own faith and framework for the outsider, indeed, for many outsiders. True, people think that the most important problem confronting religion is secularity or falling away; but it is clear from all studies, religious affiliation remains constant. Not only so, but when we look at the evidence of our own eyes, we find the vital signs of religion attested in the headlines everyday: Christian civil war in Ireland, monotheist civil war in the Middle East, the breakup of the Soviet Empire by reason of religious conflict—these attest to the power of religion. They also remind us of its pathos, which is the incapacity of religions to form for themselves a useful theory of the other. That, not secularization, defines the critical task facing religions: their excess of success in persuading the believers so that believers not only love one another, they hate everybody else.

The commonplace theory of religious systems concerning the other or the outsider, consigning to incomprehensibility the different and the other, finds ample illustration here. What do you do with the outsider? Find the other crazy (as we did Ayatollah Khomeini and Jim Jones of Jonestown), or declare the other the work of the devil (as the Ayatollah did with us), or consign the other subject to such metaphors as unclean, impure, dangerous, to be exterminated, as the Germans—Christians, ex-Christians alike—did with the Jews. In the case of the tragedy unfolding at Auschwitz, the theory of the other is difficult to express; I am confident that the Carmelite Sisters have only good will for all persons, and I am equally certain that the Jewish survivors, bearers of the moral heritage of the Jewish people and of Judaism in this setting, bear no ill will for Christianity. The one side identifies the site in its framework and in its terms, the other in its context, and neither seems to have the capacity to grasp the viewpoint of the other within its own frame of reference. Therein lies a future of not merely intolerance or misunderstanding, but of utter incomprehension. And it is that incomprehension of the other, the inability to explain the other to oneself in one's own terms, that transforms religion from a force for peace and reconciliation into a cause of war and intolerance.

Tolerance does not suffice. A theory of the other that concedes the outsider is right for the other but not for me invokes a meretricious relativism that religious believers cannot really mean. Religions will have to learn how to think about the other, not merely to tolerate the other as an unavoidable inconvenience or an evil that cannot be eliminated. For reasons I shall explain, they face the task of thinking, within their own theological framework and religious system, about the place within the structure of the other outside of it. And that is something no religion has ever accomplished up to this time.

Religions have spent their best intellectual energies in thinking about themselves, not about the outsider. Why should this be so? The reason is that religions form accounts of a social world, the one formed by the pious; they set forth a world view, define a way of life that realizes that world view, and identify the social entity that constitutes the world explained by the world view and embodied in the way of life: world without end. The this-worldly power of religion derives from its capacity to hold people together and make them see themselves not as a given but a gift: special, distinctive, chosen, saved—whatever. But the very remarkable capacity of religions to define all that is important about a person, a family, a group also incapacitates religions in a world in which difference must be accommodated. For in explaining the social world within, religions also build walls against the social world without, and in consequence religions impose upon the other, the outsider, a definition and a standing that scarcely serve the social order and the public interest.

For theories of "the other" that afford at best toleration, at worst humiliation and subordination, may have served in an age of an ordered society, but they do not fit a time in which social change forms the sole constant. It is one thing to design a hierarchical society defined by religion when one religion is on top, all others subordinated, as was the case in the Islamic nation(s) from the seventh century and as was the case in Christian Europe until the rise of the nation-state. A hierarchy based upon religion—with Islam at the apex, and with Christianity and Judaism tolerated, but on the whole well-treated minorities—

served so long as all parties accepted their place. So, too, Christian European society before the Reformation had its dual theory of religious difference within the social order: the Christian state headed by the pope, Christ's deputy; and the monarch, the secular Christian counterpart. In such an order, Judaism found its place as testimony, Islam was kept at bay across the Pyrenees or Mediterranean and then forced back in the Near East itself, and paganism was eliminated. But with the shaking of the foundations in the Reformation, for instance, the social order trembled. Christianity in the West became two, then many, and the hiarchical structure tottered. Then what of the other? Jews were driven to the East, to the more tolerant pioneering territories of Poland, Lithuania, White Russia, the Ukraine; Islam would then be ignored; and Christians would spend centuries killing other Christians. Some theory of the other! Some theory of the social order!

The solution of the seventeenth century was simple: the head of state defines the governing church. That served where it served. The solution of the eighteenth century was still more simple: tolerate everything, because all religions are equally ridiculous. But no religion accepted either theory of religious difference, and it was with no theory of the other that the West in the nineteenth and twentieth centuries entered its great ages of consolidation and expansion and fruition, then dissolution and civil strife. The civil war of Western then world civilization proved no age for thinking about the social order, and the pressing problem of religious accommodation of religious difference hardly gained attention. The reason is that from 1914 to nearly the present day, it was by no means clear that humanity would survive the civil war fought at such cost and for so long. With a million killed in one battle in 1915, with twenty million Soviet citizens killed in World War II after a prior ten million Soviet citizens were killed by their own government in the decade preceding the war, with six million Jews murdered in factories built to manufacture death—with humanity at war with itself, religions could hardly be expected to reconsider long-neglected and scarcely urgent questions.

Yet it is obvious that religious theories of religious difference— theories formed within the framework of a religious world view, way of life, and social entity—about those beyond that framework, do impose upon us an urgent task now. Part of the reason is the simple fact that we have survived the twentieth century. In 1945 no one knew we would, and many doubted it. But the atomic peace is holding, and while the competition between the United States and the Soviet Union may take other forms, the threat of armed conflict on a global scale has diminished.

That adventitious fact by itself would hardly precipitate deep thought within religion on the requirements of the social order: how to get along with the outsider. But a more important fact does. It is that the two hundred year campaign against religion on the part of forces of secularization has simply failed. Faith in God, worship of God, life with God—these testimonies to the vitality of religions are measurable: people go to church or synagogue, they observe this rite and that requirement, they make their pilgrimages, and by these quite objective measures of the fact of human action the vast majority of most of the nations of the world is made up of religious believers of one kind or another. All claims that secularization is the established and one-way process and the demise of religion forms the wave of the future have defied the facts of religious power and (alas) worldly glory. Not only is religion strong in its own realm, religious affiliations and commitments define loyalties and concerns in the larger social world of politics and culture. Anyone who doubts it had better try to explain without religion the intense opposition to abortion manifested by from one-third to nearly one-half (depending on the framing of the issue) of the voting population of this country— like it or not. In the formation of social groups, for instance, religion remains a critical indicator as to where we live, how we choose our friends, whom we marry.

That brings us back to the century rushing toward us, an age of parlous peace, a time in which, for the first time in human history, we have the opportunity of a period of sustained peace— but only if . . . We can have peace on earth only if we find sources of good will for one another, for in the end, moved by hatred, we may well bring down upon ourselves the roof of the temple that is over us all. Hatred of the other, after all, forms a powerful motive to disregard love of self, and anyone who doubts that fact had better reconsider the history of Germany from July 1944 through May 1945. At that time, when everyone knew the German cause was finished, hatred of the other sufficed to sustain a suicidal war that ended with the absolute ruin of all Germany; more people died in the last nine months of World War II than in the first five years. All that kept Germany going on the path to its own complete destruction was hatred: drag them all down with us. So much for the power of hatred. There is, then, no guarantee, despite the *pax atomica* that protects us now, of a long-term peace. There is good reason to tremble when we consider how hatred, brewed within religious theories of the other as the devil, for example, leads nations to act contrary to all rational interest; the recent war between Iraq and Iran suffices to prove that point.

So there really is a considerable and urgent task before religions today, the task of addressing a question long thought settled by the various religious systems that now flourish. It is the question of the other. And the question is to be framed in terms that only religions can confront, that is, the *theological* theory of the other. The theological question of the other has been framed in these terms: how, as a believing person, can I make sense of the outsider? For a long time that had to suffice. But now we have to reframe the question: How, as a believing person, can I make sense of the outsider with not mere tolerance of different but esteem for a faith not my own?

To expand the question, How can I form a theory of the other in such a way that within my own belief I can respect the other and accord to the outsider legitimacy within the structure of my own faith?

I say very simply that no Western religious tradition has ever answered those questions. None has tried. The hierarchical theory of religions has served, by which Islam at the apex made room for Christianity and Judaism and eliminated everything else; or Christianity at the apex (always in theory, sometimes in practice) found a cave, a cleft in the rock, for Judaism, kept Islam out of sight, and eliminated everything else. Judaism for its part expressed its hierarchical counterpart by assigning to undifferentiated humanity (Islam and Christianity never singled out for special handling) a set of requirements for a minimal definition of a humane and just social order, with holy Israel, God's first love, responsible for everything else. Of you God wants civility;

of us, holiness — a hierarchy with one peak and a vast flat plain, no mountain of ascent in between.

When we take note of how religions in the past and present have thought about the other, we may perceive the full weight of the task that is now incumbent upon us. Looking backward, all our models tell us what not to do, but we have scarcely a single model to emulate. A Christian theology of the other in terms of the other for faithful Christians; a Judaic theology of the other in terms of the other for believing Jews — these have no precedent in either Christian or Judaic theology. That effort at treating as legitimate and authentic a religion other than our own and treating religious people different from ourselves as worthy of respect because of their religion, we have never seen on this earth before, though in the past quarter century the beginnings of the work have been attempted — so far as I know solely by Roman Catholic and mainstream Protestant theologians.

I assign to the future the task of thinking about a religious theory of the other, because I can find in the past no suitable examples of how that thought might unfold or what rules of intellect may govern. In the case of Judaism, for example, Judaism thought about Christianity when, in the fourth century, it was forced to do so. In the case of one Christianity, the British one, Christianity thought about Buddhism when, in the nineteenth century, it found it required a theory to make sense of chaotic facts. In both cases, we see religions thinking about the other solely in terms of themselves.

The case of Judaism tells us when and why a religion must frame a theory of the other. It is when political change of a fundamental character transfigures the social world that a religious system addresses, thus imposing an urgent question that must be addressed. In the case of Judaism that change, at once political and religious, came about when in the fourth century Christianity became the religion of the Roman Empire. At that moment, the new faith, long ignored as a petty inconvenience at best, required attention, and more to the point, the fundamental allegations of the new faith, all of them challenges to Judaism, demanded response. Christians had long told Israel that Jesus is Christ, that the Messiah has come, and that there is no further salvation awaiting Israel; that Christians were now bearers of the promises of the Old Testament, and in them, the Israelite prophets' predictions were realized; that Christians were now Israel and Israel was now finished. The political change in government made it necessary for the people of Israel, particularly in the Land of Israel ("Palestine"), to respond to Christianity as in the prior three centuries they had not had to.

What they did by way of response was not to form a theory of Christianity within the framework of Judaism, but to re-form their theory of Judaism—of who is Israel and what is its relationship, through the Torah, with God. To that theory, Christendom was simply beside the point. Within that theory—that religious system defining the holy way of life, world view, and social entity that was Israel—Christianity did not find any explanation at all. Nor has it ever since. But at least, for a brief moment, Judaism thought about Christianity. Forced by political change, that stunning shift in the political circumstance of a religion affected that religion's thought about, among other enduring questions, the outsider, the other, the brother, and the enemy. And as a matter of fact, in thinking about the other, that same religion reconsidered the enduring and long-settled issues concerning itself as well. The fact that thinking about the other means we have also to rethink the truth about ourselves explains, I think, why we are so reluctant to do so.

So far I have argued that people talk about the same things when they have to, and that they talk about the same things also because they can. When they do so, what sort of discourse emerges? One answer to that question derives from Western theories of Buddhism as shaped by British Christianity in the nineteenth century. When the British encountered Buddhism, now in the imperial age of the nineteenth century, they faced a formidable task. It was both to make sense and to justify: to make sense of a continuing presence, to justify their own presence within the Buddhist world. Philip C. Almond just now has demonstrated a fact that, so far as I know, none has appreciated before, which is that the very concept of "Buddhism" is an invention of the West. He says, "there was an imaginative creation of Buddhism in the first half of the nineteenth century, and . . . the Western creation of Buddhism progressively enabled certain aspects of Eastern Cultures to be defined, delimited, and classified. . . . the reification of the term 'Buddhism' . . . defined the nature and content of this entity."[2]

Almond's point is that, while thinking they were discovering Buddhism, in fact Western scholars were inventing it. For they formed a category of their own choosing so as to join and homogenize a vast variety of data that, in their own setting, were differentiated and not harmonized. Scholarship on Buddhism then forms a chapter in the Western response to the world made necessary by imperialism. As Western nations conquered foreign lands and took them over, they had to answer two questions: [1] What is this? and [2] Why is it mine? The first question demanded making sense of nonsense, that is, of the unfamiliar; the second asked an equally nonsensical question: What am I doing here? The way in which the first question was answered differed from the medieval theory of the other. The medieval Christians looked for analogies to make the other familiar. The modern ones simply made the other familiar by remaking it into their own image, after their own likeness. Being scholars, they not only organized, they also selected the data with which they could conveniently cope, which is to say, books they could bring home, publish, and study in their libraries.

Almond proves, in his language, "Buddhism was reified as a textual object. By the middle of the Victorian period, Buddhism was seen as essentially constituted by its textuality, and it was the Buddhism thus constructed and thus interpreted that was the criterion against which its manifestations in the 'Orient' were measured, and generally . . . found wanting. A crucial product of this process of the textualization of Buddhism was the emergence of the historical Buddha. By the middle of the Victorian period the Buddha had emerged from the wings of myth and entered the historical stage. No longer identified with the ancient gods, distinct from the Hindu account of him and his mythical predecessors, the Buddha was a human figure—one to be compared not with the gods but with other historical personalities, and one to be interpreted in the light of the Victorian ideal of humanity."[3] So, in a word, in developing a theory of the other, the British invented Buddhism, defined it as a textual object, published the texts, in all, "determined the framework in which Buddhism was imaginatively constructed, not only for themselves, but also in the

final analysis for the East itself. . . . this was an aspect of the
Western creation of two qualitatively different modes of being
human, the oriental and the occidental . . . This fundamental
mode of organizing the East [provided a] conceptual filter through
which acceptable aspects of Buddhism could be endorsed, unac-
ceptable ones rejected."[4]

What we see is that the British intellectuals solved the problem
of the other by making the other over into the self. These
certainties, these self-evident truths and obviously valid judgments—all constituted a re-presentation of the other into the self.
And that is at its foundations not vastly different from the fourth-
century Judaic intellectuals' confrontation of the other wholly in
terms of the self, and the thirteenth-century Christian intellectuals' reading of the other wholly in terms of self. That is
what people do, the difference between the religious fourth—and
thirteenth-century versions of the secular nineteenth-century
version being only the honesty and innocence of the former times,
as against the ineffable snobbery of the moderns. Judaic theology
did not like Christianity, but it did not hold it in contempt and it
did not reinvent it; Christian theology did not like Buddhism,
but while misinterpreting through miscast analogies, it did not
fabricate it; but the British intellectuals of the nineteenth century
made up the other in their own image, after their own likeness—
and in their own studies, turned into factories for the manufacture
of mass-produced others, all of them in the model of the self.

That brings us back to our own time, which is, after all, not the
twentieth but the twenty-first century. Ours is an intellectual task,
for if we cannot in a rational and rigorous way think religiously
about the other, then the good works of politics and the ordering
of society will not be done. And the dimensions of our task are
formidable. For we have seen what does not serve. Tolerance
works only in a climate of indifference; when you care, so it seems,
you also hate. Toleration works where law prevails, but the limits
of the law are set by sovereign power, and the range of difference
on the other side of the border stretches to the last horizon. So are
we able in wit and imagination, mind and intellect, to form a
theory of the other coherent with the entire structure of the world
that our religious world view, way of life, account of the "us" that
is the social entity, comprise? The issue of coherence is critical,

and that matter of cogency with the whole religious system explains why at stake are theological propositions. Tolerance is a mere social necessity, but we all recognize, simply not a theological virtue. Anyone who doubts should recall the ridicule that met the position, "It does not matter what you believe, as long as you're a good person," not to mention, "It does not matter what you believe, as long as you believe something."

Beyond tolerance and before theology—that is where we now stand. The history of religion is teaching us about the failures of the past, so closing off paths that lead nowhere. Can religious systems make sense of what lies beyond the system? In my judgment the answer must be affirmative, because the question comes with urgency.

Where to begin? I think it is with the recognition of the simple fact that the world really is different beyond its difference from us. By that I mean, religious systems differentiate within, but homogenize the world beyond. They find it possible to conduct a detailed exegesis of their own social order, forming their own hierarchy within; but when it comes to the world beyond the limits of the system, everything is represented as pretty much the same. And that is a component of the systemic coping with difference: we are differentiated because we matter; the outside is undifferentiated because there difference is trivial. Catholics hate Protestants, and the hatred has nothing to do with us Jews; and Protestants have contempt for Catholics, leaving us out as well. And we nurture our spite, too. So difference is not only within the system, and that means systems must think about more differences than up to now they have tended to encompass.

When religious systems address the differences among outsiders, they will quite naturally reframe the question of difference in yet another way. They will not only understand that Christians are all Christians only to Jews or Muslims; but to Christians, Christians are profoundly divided. They will also understand that difference applies within: the participants of a system participate in many systems. Pluralism is existential, not only social; all of us live in many systems, working our way through many worlds, mostly serial worlds, but sometimes synchronous ones. I am not quite sure how any of us holds together the worlds of work and home, vocation and avocation, or the considerable range of loyalties that divide our hearts. But most of us do. Then, in this context, we are not only systemically Judaic or Christian or Buddhist. We are systemically defined within other frameworks as well. Those of us who are intellectuals live within one framework, with its way of life and world view and social entity; those of us who are politicians live within another, with its way of life, world view, and political class; those of us who are athletes live by yet another schedule and do other things. And so it goes, and that is to speak only of the intersecting systems of the common life. What shall we then say of home and family and its confusion? In all, the happy chaos of our lives belies the neat and orderly hierarchy that religious systems impute to the social world. Whether or not in times past people lived so neatly ordered I cannot say, but today they do not. Religion matters not only because it integrates; it matters because it is one of the sole media of integration left to us. For all of its power to define who we are and what we want to be and to what "us" we belong, religion too forms only one circle—concentric, perhaps, with more of the circles of our lives than others, but coexistent with the lives of only a few specialists. For the rest, religious difference is just another difference. Now that is something for theology to think about. And when theology addresses difference within, then quite naturally a theory of difference beyond will take shape.

This, then, is a time for intellectuals to do their work courageously. The events at Oswiecim have turned a chronic into an acute problem, and it will be a *Qiddush Hasham*—an act, like the act of martyrdom, that is a sanctification of the name of God—on the part of religious intellectuals, both Judaic and Christian ones, to meet that challenge as an urgent example of an enduring religious dilemma: making sense of the other in the intellectual tools provided by one's own religion and its theology.

7

Can Judaism Make Any Sense at All of Christianity?

The Case of Mary as Mother of God

To a believing Jew, Christianity looks like Judaism; yet on closer inspection it differs radically, and consequently, the Christian family of religions is exceedingly difficult to understand. If Christianity were wholly unlike Judaism, then any dialogue with Christianity on the part of Judaism would begin with the recognition that the other is wholly other: beyond all parallels, comparisons, and contrasts. Whether and how then to conduct religious dialogue on religious issues is to be worked out from the starting point of utter incomprehensibility. The same is so for Christianity in regard to Judaism. Every Christian knows about Judaism, and what Christians know is wrong. For Christians commonly suppose that Judaism is the religion of the Old Testament, but that is only partly true—therefore wholly false. The root of the difficulty in seeing similarities where there is none, of course, is that both religions appeal to the same writing. Christianity appeals to the Old Testament, in contrast to the New Testament, as part of the Bible; Judaism appeals to the written Torah, in contrast to the oral Torah, as part of the one whole Torah given by God at Mt. Sinai to Moses, our rabbi. Since we revere as God's word some of the same writings, we take for granted that we form a single family. So, we assume, we ought to be able to understand one another. And we take for granted that when we speak, we are going to be understood, and when we listen, we are going to understand.

But that is not how things have been in our own times. Here we face a formulation of the dialogue between Judaism as a religion and Christianity as a religion in which a surface conversation covers over profound mutual incomprehension. If I may summarize the prevailing theory of the dialogue, it is that Jesus was a Jew and therefore, in order to understand Christianity, Christians must come to terms with Judaism. Important schools of New Testament studies, aiming to identify those sayings of Jesus that really were said by him, have excluded the sayings that they deem unjudaic, and still more important circles of New Testament scholarship appeal to Judaic sources as a principal source of hermeneutics. One theological position then distinguishes between the Jesus of history, who was born, lived, and died as a Jew, and the Christ of theology. The connection to the dialogue between Judaism and Christianity is then simple. The two religions can speak with one another because Christianity derives from Judaism through the person of Jesus, a historical figure. If, then, we wish to understand Christianity, we peel back the layers of "inauthentic" theology and reach back into the core and heart, the Judaism of Jesus then forming authentic Christianity. Judaism then may be represented in such a way as to reject the rest of the Judaism of that time or place; Jesus vastly reformed what there was; Christianity then is what Judaism ought to have become. The upshot is a dialogue with Judaism that yields an apologetic for Christianity and a condemnation of Judaism as we know it—not much better than the medieval disputations produced, hardly a model of a genuine interchange of religions attempting to take one another seriously.

Nor has Judaism contributed a more suitable example of how to take seriously another religion in terms of one's own religion. If there is no Christian theology of Judaism, at least some have made the effort, building, for instance, on Paul in Romans 9. But apart from a feeble effort of Rosenzweig to postulate a dual covenant—Christianity for the Gentiles, Judaism for holy Israel—no Judaic theology of Christianity has founded a theological tradition of breadth and weight (although a serious interesting Judaic Christology should not be ignored). In general, the Judaic approach to a theory of Christianity treats that religion within the metaphor of a family, as "the daughter faith"; or it regards that religion with condescension ("for the Gentiles" indeed!—along with pork and shell fish, I assume); or it deems only the historical Jesus (not the theological Christ) as worthy of serious attention. The apologetic claim of Judaism in its modern and contemporary formulation, moreover, has rested upon the allegation that Judaism sets forth the real, the historical meaning of the scriptures of ancient Israel, and Christianity, self-evidently, does not. That is to say, no one can imagine Isaiah really had the Virgin Mary in mind when he spoke of the virgin or the young woman who would conceive; or that Isaiah spoke of Jesus Christ when he prophesied about the suffering servant. So, since the prophets did not prophesy about Jesus Christ—such being (so the apologetic in scholarly guise maintains) impossible—Judaism conveys the authentic faith of ancient Israel. The beam in the hermeneutical eye of Judaism, of course, is the Judaic hermeneutic supplied by the Midrash compilations of ancient times, which impart to the scriptures of ancient Israel a rich and contemporary meaning, no more the plain sense of the ancient writers than the Christian one of Matthew.

It seems to me only when Christianity can see itself in the way in which the Church fathers saw it—as new and uncontingent, a complete revision of the history of humanity from Adam onward, not as a subordinate and heir of Judaism—and when Judaism can see itself in the way in which the sages of the oral Torah saw it—as the statement of God's Torah for all humanity—that the two religions will recognize this simple fact: they really are totally alien to one another. Dialogue will begin with the recognition of difference, with a search for grounds for some form of communication, rather than with the assumption of sameness and the search for commonalities. People wish to read the Gospels, in particular, in the context of Judaism and the sources of Judaism of that time and place. But much that the Gospel narrative takes for granted proves surprising to a Jewish reader. Just now, for example, someone asked me about burial practice in the first century. I replied that I have no evidence from the rabbinic sources that pertains to that time in particular, but in general, in later times, the men took care of the men, the women of the women. What then am I to make of the story of how women tended the body of Jesus? That seems to me quite surprising. I wonder whether anyone before found it so. But we find Christianity truly surprising when we accord to it its proper autonomous standing: Christianity came into being as a surprising, unprecedented, and entirely autonomous religious system and structure, not as a child, whether legitimate or otherwise, of Judaism.

The representation of Jesus in the Gospels constantly surprises, even amazes one familiar with other reports of the Judaism of the time—just as the authors of the Gospels said. But then what is a Judaic believer to make of Christianity? When Jesus contrasted his teaching with what others had been saying, he underlined this simple point: the Christ of theology begins with the Jesus of history. Jesus was Jesus Christ in the Gospels and to the evangelists as much as he was Christ Jesus to Paul; any distinction between the Jesus of history and the Christ of faith, whether invidious or favorable, ignores not only the explicit claims of the Gospels themselves but also the genuinely surprising character of the representation of Jesus in the context of any Judaism known to us today. The characterization of Jesus as a Galilean wonder worker like Honi the Circle Drawer, for example, is a total fabrication, a deliberate misreading of the Gospels, and a distortion of the very character of the rabbinic evidence adduced in behalf of that proposition. Where does this leave us? Is there no bridge from Christianity "back" to Judaism, and is there no connection that links Judaism to Christianity? My argument is that there is none, there should be none, and when we recognize that the two are utterly distinct and different families of religions, the work of attempting a dialogue can begin.

Then how do I propose to proceed from this ground zero that I claim forms our common location? Let me begin the work of defining a new foundation for dialogue by making one point only. It is that the only way for a Judaic believer to understand Christianity is within Judaic terms, and the only way for a Christian believer to understand Judaism is within Christian terms. Since Judaism and Christianity form quite different religions with little in common, it is time for each religion to try to make sense of the other—but to make sense of the stranger wholly in one's own terms. Can I, as a Jew and a believer in Judaism, understand in my context, in my terms of faith, the religion of the Christian? Can I frame a Judaic religious under-

standing of the religion of Christianity? What it means to understand another religion demands a definition. Up to now, as I
already have noted, some rather unsuccessful efforts at theologies,
each of the other, have shown us what not to attempt: a Christian
theology of Judaism proves, if not condescending, then unchristian—conceding more than Christianity has ever conceded in the
past; a Judaic theology of Christianity gives no less and no more
authentically. Judaism cannot concede that Jesus Christ is what
the Christians say, and any other judgment upon Jesus Christ is
simply beside the point. Christianity may concede that we retain
our covenanted relationship with God, but it cannot then admit
that converts to Judaism have taken the right route to salvation.
So all that Christianity concedes is that Judaism is all right for
the Jews, a concession to be sure, but not of vast consequence.

If not a theological understanding of one another, then what
other understanding can we seek? My answer derives from the
commonplace fact that, after all, we really do worship one God,
who is the same God, and who is the only God, we and the
Muslims with us. Within that common ground of being, a human
task before us emerges. It is to seek in the religious experience of
the other, the stranger and outsider, that with which we within
our own world can identify.

But how are we to do this? Let me give a single example of what
it will take. It involves the figure of the Virgin, because that is a
person critical to Roman Catholic and Orthodox Christianity and
exceedingly difficult for a Judaic believer to understand in Judaic
terms. The notion of a woman with a special claim on God's
attention—how am I as a Jew to grasp this? The answer is by
finding in my own tradition an analogy that will tell me what, in
my context, Mary stands for in her context. Jews have trouble
enough dealing with Jesus in the Christian reading not of his life
and teachings, with which we can identify, but with the claim
that, in a unique way, he is God's only begotten son. What then
are we to make of Mary? Mary, after all, is called "Mother of
God" and revered and loved by Roman Catholics; she is bearer
of profound religious sentiments indeed. But if we cannot grasp
how any one man is more God's son than any other, then how can
we make sense of how any one woman is more God's mother than
any other. That is why, in the serious exchange of belief and

conviction that in our own time Roman Catholics and Jews undertake, we bypass Mary in silence. We pretend Catholics are Protestants, for whom Mary is not a critical figure, and we deny by our silence the Roman Catholic reverence for Mary, worship through Mary of the God we share with them.

To make my point, I have first to call attention to Matthew's representation of the flight into Egypt, because it will show that what I shall present as a Judàic equivalent to Mary's relationship to God is specific and particular, not general and abstract:

and going into the house they saw the child with Mary his mother, and they fell down and worshipped him . . .

An angel of the Lord appeared to Joseph in a dream and said, "Rise, take the child and his mother and flee to Egypt" . . . and he rose and took the child and his mother by night and departed to Egypt . . .

Then Herod, when he saw that he had been tricked by the wise men, was in a furious rage, and he sent and killed all the male children in Bethlehem and in all that region who were two years old or under . . . Then was fulfilled what was spoken by the prophet, Jeremiah:

> "A voice was heard in Ramah,
> wailing and loud lamentation,
> Rachel weeping for her children;
> she refused to be consoled,
> because they were no more."

When Herod died, behold, an angel of the Lord appeared in a dream to Joseph in Egypt, saying, "Rise, take the child and his mother and go to the land of Israel, for those who sought the child's life are dead."

And he rose and took the child and his mother and went to the land of Israel.

Matt. 2:11, 13-14, 16-21

What is important here is that Mary is represented as a figure much like Rachel, protecting her children and weeping for them. The flight to Egypt in the story of Jesus is represented as a counterpart to the Exile of Israel in the time of Jeremiah; Jesus stands for Jeremiah and Mary for Rachel, in Matthew's account.

Now in my own studies in preparation for the dialogue with Father Andrew Greeley that has now yielded *Our Bible: A Priest and a Rabbi Read the Scripture Together*, I have found a figure in the Judaic reading of the Bible that stands in Judaism for some of the things that, in Roman Catholic Christianity, Mary represents. So the capacity of Roman Catholic Christians to revere Mary, the power of Mary to arouse in Catholic hearts and souls a greater love for God than they would otherwise feel—the response to Mary and the power of Mary seem not so alien as they did before. For what Mary stands for is a woman who bears a special, a unique relationship to God, a relationship so compelling that God will respond to Mary in a way in which God will not respond to any other person. So when I ask myself, Do we have, in the Judaic reading of scripture, a figure that can show me how a woman may accomplish with God what no man can do? I, of course, find the answer ready at hand. Once I have asked the question in that way, Do we have in Judaism a counterpart to Mary, a live and lovely woman to whom God listens, whose prayers carry weight more than any man's? the answer is self-evident.

And curiously, the Judaic Mary plays a critical role in the very passage in which Mary and Jesus figure as principals. The story of the birth of Jesus to the Virgin Mary draws attention to the one figure in the Hebrew scripture that provides a counterpart, and not only so, but the very way in which Mary's ancient Israelite counterpart enters the tale is exactly the way in which, in the ancient sages' reading of scripture, Rachel plays her part. Mary in the gospel of Matthew flees with Joseph and the infant Jesus into exile. As she goes into exile, so the first Gospel indicates, there is weeping for the slaughter of the infant children, and the one who weeps is Rachel.

Now to the Judaic reader, the story of exile, slaughter, and mourning involving Rachel is strikingly familiar. For we find in the rabbinic reading of the Book of Lamentation, in the work Lamentations Rabbah, a closely parallel account. Indeed, the intervention of Rachel in the story at hand runs so close to the Roman Catholic conception of the Virgin's power to intervene and intercede that, understanding and feeling the anguish of Rachel, I can reach out also to the Roman Catholic capacity to invoke the power of Mary, virgin and saint, in her special relationship to God.

Lest these statements seem extravagant, let me forthwith lay out the representation of Rachel and her special power before God. What is important to me in this presentation is not merely that Rachel weeps for Israel going into exile, the way Rachel weeps in the First Gospel for the slaughter of the innocents as Joseph, Mary, and Jesus go into exile. That parallel is interesting and illuminating but not to the point. What I find striking is the parallel between Rachel's unique relationship to God and Mary's unique relationship to God. For that is something we Jews are not accustomed to noting, and yet, here it is.

> R. Samuel bar Nahmani said, "[When God contemplated destroying the Temple and sending the Israelites in Exile to Babylon,] Abraham forthwith commenced speaking before the Holy One, blessed be he, saying to him, 'Lord of the world, when I was a hundred years old, you gave me a son. And when he had already reached the age of volition, a boy thirty-seven years of age, you told me,' offer him up as a burnt-offering before me!"
>
> "And I turned mean to him and had no mercy for him, but I myself tied him up. Are you not going to remember this and have mercy on my children?"
>
> "Isaac forthwith commenced speaking before the Holy One, blessed be he, saying to him, 'Lord of the world, when father said to me, "God will see to the lamb for the offering for himself, my son" (Gen. 22:8), I did not object to what you had said, but I was bound willingly, with all my heart, on the altar, and spread forth my neck under the knife. Are you not going to remember this and have mercy on my children!'
>
> "Jacob forthwith commenced speaking before the Holy One, blessed be he, saying to him, 'Lord of the world, did I not remain in the house of Laban for twenty years? And when I went forth from his house, the wicked Esau met me and wanted to kill my children, and I gave myself over to death in their behalf. Now my children are handed over to their enemies like sheep for slaughter, after I raised them like fledglings of chickens. I bore on their account the anguish of raising children,

for through most of my life I was pained greatly on their account. And now are you not going to remember this and have mercy on my children!'

"Moses forthwith commenced speaking before the Holy One, blessed be he, saying to him, 'Lord of the world, was I not a faithful shepherd for the Israelites for forty years? I ran before them in the desert like a horse. And when the time came for them to enter the land, you issued a decree against me in the wilderness that there my bones would fall. And now that they have gone into exile, you have sent to me to mourn and weep for them.'

"Then Moses said to Jeremiah, 'Go before me, so I may go and bring them in and see who will lay a hand on them.'

"Said to him Jeremiah, 'It isn't even possible to go along the road, because of the corpses.'

"He said to him, 'Nonetheless.'

"Forthwith Moses went along, with Jeremiah leading the way, until they came to the waters of Babylon.

"They saw Moses and said to one another, 'Here comes the son of Amram from his grave to redeem us from the hand of our oppressors.'

"An echo went forth and said, 'It is a degree from before me.'

"Then said Moses to them, 'My children, to bring you back is not possible, for the decree has already been issued. But the Omnipresent will bring you back quickly.' Then he left them.

"Then they raised up their voices in weeping until the sound rose on high: 'By the rivers of Babylon there we sat down, yes, we wept' (Ps. 137:1).

"When Moses got back to the fathers of the world, they said to him, 'What have the enemies done to our children?'

"He said to them, 'Some of them he killed, the hands of some of them he bound behind their back, some of them he put in iron chains, some of them he stripped naked, some of them died on the way, and their corpses were left for the vultures of heaven and the hyenas of the earth, some of them were left for the sun, starving and thirsting.'

"Then they began to weep and sing dirges: 'Woe for what has happened to our children! How have you become orphans without a father! How have you had to sleep in the hot sun during the summer without clothes and covers! How have you had to walk over rocks and stones without shoes and sandals! How were you burdened with heavy bundles of sand! How were your hands bound behind your backs! How were you left unable even to swallow the spit in your mouths!'

"Moses then said, 'Cursed are you, O sun! Why did you not grow dark when the enemy went into the house of the sanctuary?'

"The sun answered him, 'By your life, Moses, faithful shepherd! They would not let me nor did they leave me alone, but beat me with sixty whips of fire, saying, "Go, pour out your light."'

"Moses then said, 'Woe for your brilliance, O Temple, how has it become darkened? Woe that its time has come to be destroyed, for the building to be reduced to ruins, for the school children to be killed, for their parents to go into captivity and exile and the sword!'

"Moses then said, 'O you who have taken the captives! I impose an oath on you by your lives! If you kill, do not kill with a cruel form of death, do not exterminate them utterly, do not kill a son before his father, a daughter before her mother, for the time will come for the Lord of heaven to exact a full reckoning from you!'

"The wicked Chaldeans did not do things this way, but they brought a son before his mother and said to the father, 'Go, kill him!' The mother wept, her tears flowing over him, and the father hung his head.

"And further Moses said before him, 'Lord of the world! You have written in your Torah, "Whether it is a cow or a ewe, you shall not kill it and its young both in one day" ' (Lev. 22:28).

"But have they not killed any number of children along with their mothers, and yet you remain silent!'

"Then Rachel, our mother, leapt to the fray and said to the Holy One, blessed be he, 'Lord of the world! It is perfectly self-evident to you that your servant, Jacob, loved me with a mighty love, and worked for me for father for seven years, but when those seven years were fulfilled, and the time came for my wedding to my husband, father planned to substitute my sister for me in the marriage to my husband.

"Now that matter was very hard for me, for I knew the deceit, and I told my husband and gave him a sign by which he would know the difference between me and my sister, so that my father would not be able to trade me off. But then I regretted it and I bore my passion, and I had mercy for my sister, that she should not be shamed. So in the evening for my husband they substituted my sister for me, and I gave my sister all the signs that I had given to my husband, so that he would think that she was Rachel.

"And not only so, but I crawled under the bed on which he was lying with my sister, while she remained silent, and I made all the replies so that he would not discern the voice of my sister.

"I paid my sister only kindness, and I was not jealous of her, and I did not allow her to be shamed, and I am a mere mortal, dust and ashes. Now I had no envy of my rival, and I did not place her at risk for shame and humiliation.

"But you are the King, living and enduring and merciful. How come then you are jealous of idolatry, which is nothing, and so have sent my children into exile, allowed them to be killed by the sword, permitted the enemy to do whatever they wanted to them?!'

"Forthwith the mercy of the Holy One, blessed be he, welled up, and he said, 'For Rachel I am going to bring the Israelites back to their land.'

"That is in line with this verse of Scripture: 'Thus said the Lord: A cry is heard in Ramah, wailing, bitter weeping, Rachel weeping for her children. She refuses to be comforted for her children, who are gone. Thus said the Lord, Restrain your voice from weeping, your eyes from shedding tears; for there is a reward for your labor, declares the Lord; they shall return from the enemy's land, and there is hope for your future, declares the Lord: your children shall return to their country.' "

(Jer.31:15-17)

What I find striking in this story is how very much Rachel is like Mary (or Mary like Rachel), that is, the one who succeeds when all other intervention fails. Abraham, Isaac, Jacob, and Moses — the four most important figures in the firmament of Judaism — all make appeals that God forgive the Israelites who had sinned and not take them into exile and destroy their holy city and temple.

Nothing much happens. The holy men are told by an implacable God, "It is a degree from before me." All the people can hope for is that in due course, when the sin is expiated by suffering, God will be reconciled with them and restore them to the land.

Moses has to report this back to "the fathers of the world," Abraham, Isaac, and Jacob. The dirge then rises, curses of nature's witnesses to Israel's catastrophe. And this yields the climax: "And yet you (namely, God) remain silent." Rachel speaks in the same manner as the fathers of the world—Abraham, Isaac, and Jacob. But she speaks not of sacrifice but of love, invoking her power of expressing love for her sister through self-restraint and self-sacrifice. This address of Rachel's introduces into the argument with God what the men had not invoked, which is, the relationships within the family. Rachel's message to God is to relate to Israel with the love that comes from within the family, the holy family. Let God love Israel as much as Rachel had loved Leah. Should Rachel not have been jealous? She should have been. Did she not have the right to demand justice for herself? She did. Yet look at Rachel.

Rachel's message goes on to God; if I could do it, so can you. Why this excess of jealousy for idolatry, which is nothing, that "you have sent my children into exile?" Enough already. And God responds not to Abraham, Isaac, Jacob, Moses, or Jeremiah, but to Rachel: "For Rachel I am going to bring the Israelites back to their land." And he did. "Stop crying, Rachel, enough already: your children shall return to their country." So too as Joseph, Mary, and Jesus go into exile, Rachel weeps, and the result is the same: the family will come home and does come home.

That's why I can find in Mary a Christian, a Roman Catholic Rachel, whose prayers count when the prayers of great men, fathers of the world, fall to the ground. God listens to the mother, God responds to her plea, because—so Hosea has it, among so many of the prophets—God's love for us finds its analogy and counterpart in the love of the husband for the wife and the wife for the husband and the mother for the children, above all. No wonder when Rachel weeps, God listens. How hard, then, can it be for me to find in Mary that sympathetic, special friend that Roman Catholics have known for two thousand years! Not so hard at all. So yes, if Rachel, then why not Mary? But then, as I have become fluent in Catholic (and speak pretty decent Protestant, too), that now seems to me self-evident.

Is this just a scholastic point about parallels? I hope not. My point is just the opposite. My problem with Mary, the heart of Roman Catholic Christianity, is how to find a way of understanding with empathy what Roman Catholics say, and more to the point, how they feel about Mary. If the Roman Catholic faith centers, upon a figure that is wholly other, with whom I cannot identify, for whom in my own experience I can find no counterpart, then in the end I can never make sense of the things Roman Catholic Christians cherish. But if I can say yes, in your world, your path leads you to the feet of Mary; and coming out of my world, I can follow that quest and that yearning of yours, then there can be sympathy, perhaps even empathy. The importance of Rachel for me in this context is that in her I can find that counterpart and model of the woman who has God's ear. Then Roman Catholic Christianity in its reverence for the Virgin faith is no longer wholly other. It is not my own, never was, never can be. But it is a faith I can grasp, try to understand, learn to perceive with respect as a road to God, to the same God who gave me the Torah at Sinai and to whom I said at Sinai, in Israel the holy people: "We shall do and we shall obey." That God who demands obedience, hears the voice of Rachel. So why not Mary? The two religions are utterly different, bearing different messages and distinctive meanings, each for its own faithful. Yet out of my religion I can make sense of that other, that different religion. And that seems to me to define the task for the coming century, in which, for the first time in two millennia, good will joins Christians and Jews in the service of the one God—whom alone we now serve—for the first time ever, together.

8

Judaism and Christianity

The Bavli and the Bible

Why the Talmud Matters

My insistence that the two religions, Judaism and Christianity, communicate only with great imprecision, if at all, concludes with a comparison of the foundation documents of the two traditions: the Talmud of Babylonia or the Bavli, for Judaism; the Bible, consisting of the Old Testament and the New Testament, for Christianity. The differences between these two documents, each definitive in its context, seem to me to demonstrate why dialogue proves so difficult to attain.

The Talmud is important because it defined, and now defines, Judaism. Christians and other Gentiles in the West take for granted that Judaism is the religion of the Old Testament, but since Judaism reads the Old Testament through the interpretation of the rabbis of the Talmud and related writings, that statement is only half true. It is, in fact, precisely as true as the statement, "Christianity is the religion of the Old Testament." Christianity reads the Old Testament in the light of the New Testament. More accurately, Christianity is the religion of the Bible, Old and New Testaments together; Judaism is the religion of the Torah—written Torah, the Hebrew scriptures, and oral Torah, culminating in the Talmud. When, therefore, we know the written Torah, we gain access to only part of the source of Judaism. The Talmud is the other part, and given its standing, the more important part.

The rabbis of the Talmud instruct Israel, the holy people, on how they are to read the Torah inclusive of the written part. The Talmud matters because it is Judaism.

Each religion defines its authority by appeal to revelation, and both religious traditions share part of the same revelation: the Old Testament and the written Torah, referring to the same writings (more or less). Christianity finds in the Bible, meaning the Old and the New Testaments, the statement of the faith by the authority of God.[1] Judaism from antiquity to our own day has identified in the Talmud of Babylonia the summa of the Torah of Sinai, joining as it does the written Torah (encompassing what Christianity knows as the Old Testament) and the oral Torah, commencing with the Mishnah. The Bible, for Christianity, and the Bavli, for Judaism, have formed the court of final appeal in issues of doctrine and (for Judaism) normative instruction on correct deed as well. Commentaries, paraphrases, amplifications have carried out that exegetical elaboration that spun out a web of relationships. The pattern of truth that, for the Bible and for the Bavli alike served to state the world view and way of life for church and Israel, respectively, furthermore was endowed with the status of revealed truth, and to the ethos and ethics of the social entity was imputed the standing of tradition.

Comparing the Bible of Christianity and the Talmud of Judaism

What difference does the Talmud make? We answer that question when we compare the Talmud with the Bible. The comparison yields perspective on the Talmud, and that perspective will shape our interpretation. The Bavli and the Bible are quite different kinds of documents. In the differences we see the choices people made when confronting pretty much the same problem. Judaism, through the Talmud (written Torah and oral Torah), and Christianity, through the Bible (Old Testament and New Testament), worked out parallel problems.

In late antiquity, from the second through the fourth centuries for orthodox, Catholic Christianity, and from the second through the seventh centuries for the Judaism of the dual Torah, the Judaic and Christian intellectuals sorted out the complex problem of relating the worlds of the then-moderns to the words of the ancients. Both groups of intellectuals claimed to present enduring traditions in that other sense I identified earlier: a fundament of truth revealed of old and handed on to us. But both sets of thinkers also brought to realization systematic and philosophical statements, which begin in first principles and rise in steady and inexorable logic to final conclusions: compositions of proportion, balance, cogency, and order.

The authors of the Talmud received two prior systems, those of the Pentateuch and the Mishnah, and formed their own as well.[2] A simple question then faced the heirs of the Pentateuch (and the rest of the Hebrew scriptures) as well as of the Mishnah and the body of Mishnah interpretation produced between 200 and ca. 400 (for the Land of Israel) and ca. 600 (for Babylonia). How can we relate the three systems—two inherited, the third invented? The solution for Judaism lay in the method of commentary, which is to say, attaching to a received text whatever one wished to say not only about that text but also in one's own name. So the solution to the problem of holding together three distinct, yet interrelated systems lay in forming the final statement that the Bavli's authorship wished to make into a commentary on the Mishnah and (through related documents of Midrash exegesis not studied in this book) on scripture alike. True, the "commentary" that bore the burden of the Bavli's system would address only those passages that the authorship of the Bavli found consequential. Equally true, the Talmud's authorship said whatever it thought important about the Mishnah and scripture, and along the way set forth its ideas on its own program as well. But that independent act of selectivity formed a principal intellectual labor of system-building.

What makes the formation of the Bavli interesting is the parallel problem facing Christian theologians in the same age. In the case of the Christianty, where do we look for a counterpart labor of system-building through selectivity? The answer, of course, is dictated by the form of the question. What we want to know is how Christianity (the church through its teaching authority) held together the entirety of an inherited corpus of writing—the Old Testament, the Gospels, the letters of the apostle Paul, and other writings deemed authoritative and holy. The answer is, by creating the Bible, Old and New Testaments together. In that work of selection, arrangement, and canonization, the church made its own statement and set forth an important component of its own system.[3] In the canonization of selected available writings into the Bible, we see the theologians' work of making choices, yielding what was deemed a cogent and single statement. When we compare the systemic structures represented by the Bavli and the Bible, therefore, we can appreciate how two quite distinct groups of intellectuals worked out solutions to a single problem, and did so, as a matter of fact, through pretty much the same medium, namely, the making of reasoned choices and the forming of the things chosen into coherent and harmonious statements of systems. There is, of course, another point in common besides the shared problem, and that is, a single solution to that problem. Specifically, both authorships set forth systems of thought, at the same time attaching to their systems the claim of tradition: God's Torah to Moses at Sinai, for Judaism, and the pattern of Christian truth, for Christianity; hence the comparison of Bavli and Bible.

The Bible and the Talmud as Statements of Systems

The points of difference are determined by the shared morphology: the Bible and the Bavli are very different ways of setting forth a system. Each represents its components in a distinctive manner: the Christian, by preserving their autonomy and calling the whole a system; the Judaic, by obscuring their originally autonomous and independent character and imparting to the whole the form of tradition. The upshot may be simply stated. The Bavli of Judaism presents what is in fact a free-standing and cogent system but imputes to it the standing of tradition. The Bible of Christianity sets forth diverse and unsystematic traditions, received writings from we know not where, and to those traditions, through the act of canonization, imputes the character and structure of a system.

To unpack these generalizations, let us turn back to the literary media in which the intellects of the two communities of intellectuals set forth their system as traditions or their traditions as system: the Bavli and the Bible, respectively. We wish specifically to see how each of these monuments of mind works out its own system, and consequently, also accomplishes the consequent tasks at hand: (1) the sorting out the issue of choosing a logic of cogent discourse to serve the interests of the system, and (2) the situating of the system in relationship to received and authoritative prior systemic statements.

The Mishnah's Systematic Mode of Discourse and Scripture

In the case of the Bavli, our point of entry is the identification of the odd mixture of logics utilized by the framers of the system as a whole. By that I mean, how did the framers of the Bavli impart cogency and coherence to the very diverse materials that they assembled in a single, continuing, and coherent statement? To set forth the distinctive logic in play in the formation of the Bavli, I must start back with the Mishnah, and still further back with scripture. For when we understand the character of the Mishnah and its relationship to the immediately prior system its authorship recognized, namely, the Pentateuch (and scripture as a whole), we shall grasp the choices confronting the Bavli's framers.

The issue of cogency presented by the Mishnah, which the Bavli in its form is arranged to serve as a vast exegesis, derives from the character of discourse in the Mishnah itself. The Mishnah utilized a single logic to set forth a system that, in form as in inner structure, stood wholly autonomous and independent, a statement unto itself with scarcely a ritual obeisance to any prior system. The Mishnah's logic of cogent discourse establishes propositions that rest upon philosophical bases, e.g., through the proposal of a thesis and the composition of a list of facts that (e.g., through shared traits of a taxonomic order) prove the thesis. The Mishnah presents rules and treats stories (inclusive of history) as incidental and of merely taxonomic interest. Its logic is propositional and its intellect does its work through a vast labor of classification, comparison, and contrast generating governing rules and generalizations. A simple contrasting case shows us that the stakes are very high. For that purpose, let us turn to a document we know our authorship knew well, namely, the written Torah. The contrast with the Pentateuch's mode of cogent discourse will show us the autonomy and the independence of the Mishnah's authorship.

The Pentateuch appeals to a different logic of cogent discourse from the Mishnah's. It is the cogency imparted by teleology, that is, a logic that provides an account of how things were in order to explain how things are, and to set forth how they should be, with the tabernacle in the wilderness the model for (and modeled after) the Temple in the Jerusalem. The Mishnah speaks in a continuing present tense, saying only how things are; it is indifferent to the *were* and the *will be*. The Pentateuch focuses upon self-conscious "Israel," saying who they were and what they must become to overcome how they now are. The Mishnah understands by "Israel" as much the individual as the nation and identifies as its principal actors, the heroes of its narrative, not the family become a nation but the priest and the householder, the woman and the slave, the adult and the child, and other castes and categories of person within an inward-looking, established, fully landed community. Given the Mishnah's authorship's interest in classifications and categories, therefore in systematic hierarchization of an orderly world, one can hardly find odd that (re)definition of the subject matter and problematic of the systemic social entity.

We may briefly dwell on this matter of difference in the prevailing logic, because the contrast allows us to see how one document will appeal to one logic, another to a different logic. While the Pentateuch appeals to the logic of teleology to draw together and make sense of facts, so making connections by appeal to the end and drawing conclusions concerning the purpose of things, the Mishnah's authorship knows only the philosophical logic of syllogism, the rule making logic of lists. The pentateuchal logic reached concrete expression in narrative, which served to point to the direction and goal of matters, hence, in the nature of things, to history. Accordingly, those authors, when putting together diverse materials, so shaped everything as to form of it all as continuous a narrative as they could construct, and through that "history" that they made up, they delivered their message and also portrayed that message as cogent and compelling.

If the pentateuchal writers were theologians of history, the Mishnah's writers aimed at composing a natural philosophy for supernatural, holy Israel. Like good Aristotelians, they would uncover the components of the rules by comparison and contrast, showing the rule for one thing by finding out how it compared with like things and contrasted with the unlike. Then, in their view, the unknown would become known, conforming to the rule of the like thing and also to the opposite of the rule governing the unlike thing.

That purpose is accomplished, in particular, through list making, which places on display the data of the like and the unlike, and implicitly (ordinarily, not explicitly) then conveys the rule. It is this resort to list making that accounts for the rhetorical stress on groups of examples of a common principle, three or five, for instance. The authorship assumes that once a series is established, the governing rule will be perceived. That explains why, in exposing the interior logic of its authorship's intellect, the Mishnah had to be a book of lists with the implicit order, the nomothetic traits of a monothetic order, dictating the ordinarily unstated general and encompassing rule.

And why all this? It is in order to make a single statement endless times over, and to repeat in a mass of tangled detail precisely the same fundamental judgment. The Mishnah in its way is as blatantly repetitious in its fundamental statement as is the Pentateuch. But the power of the pentateuchal authorship, or power denied to that of the Mishnah, lies in their capacity always to be heard, to create sound by resonance of the surfaces of things. The Pentateuch is a fundamentally popular and accessible piece of writing. By contrast, the Mishnah's writers spoke into the depths, anticipating a more acute hearing than they ever would receive. So the repetitions of scripture reinforce the message, while the endlessly repeated paradigm of the Mishnah sits too deep in the structure of the system to gain hearing from the ear that lacks acuity or to attain visibility to the untutored eye.

Turning a System into a Tradition

As soon as the Mishnah made its appearance, the vast labor of not only explaining its meaning but especially justifying its authority was sure to get under way. For the Mishnah presented one striking problem in particular. It rarely cited scriptural authority for its rules. Instead, it followed the inexorable authority of logic, specifically, the inner logic of a topic, which dictated the order of thought and defined the generative problematic that instructed its authors on what they wanted to know about a particular topic.[4] These intellectual modalities in their nature lay claim to an independence of mind, even when the result of thought is a repetition of what scripture itself says. Omitting scriptural proof texts therefore represents both silence and signals its statement. For that act of omission bore the implicit claim to an authority independent of scripture, an authority deriving from logic working within its own inner tensions and appealing to tests of reason and sound argument. In that striking fact, the document set a new course for itself. But its authorship raised problems for those who would apply its law to Israel's life.

From the formation of ancient Israelite scripture into a holy book in Judaism in the aftermath of the return to Zion and the creation of the Torah-book in Exra's time (ca. 450 B.C.E.), coming generations routinely set their ideas into relationship with scripture. This they did by citing proof texts alongside their own rules. Otherwise, in the setting of Israelite culture, the new writings could find no ready hearing. Over the six hundred years from the formation of the Torah of "Moses" in the time of Ezra, from ca. 450 B.C.E. to ca. 200 C.E. four conventional ways to accommodate new writings to the established canon of received scripture had come to the fore. First, a writer would sign a famous name to his book, attributing his ideas to Enoch, Adam, Jacob's sons, Jeremiah, Baruch, and any number of others down to Ezra. But the Mishnah bore no such attribution, e.g., to Moses. Implicitly, to be sure, the statement of M. Avot 1:1, "Moses received Torah from Sinai," carried the further notion that sayings of people on the list of authorities from Moses to nearly their own day derived from God's revelation at Sinai. But no one made that premise explicit before the time of the Bavli of the Land of Israel. Second, an authorship might also imitate the style of biblical Hebrew and so try to creep into the canon by adopting the cloak of scripture. But the Mishnah's authorship ignores biblical syntax and style. Third, an author would surely claim his work was inspired by God, a new revelation for an open canon. But, as we realize, that claim makes no explicit impact on the Mishnah. Fourth, someone would link his opinions to biblical verses through the exegesis of the latter in line with the former so that scripture would validate his views. The authorship of the Mishnah did so only occasionally, but far more commonly stated on its own authority whatever rules it proposed to lay down.

The Hebrew of the Mishnah complicated the problem because it is totally different from the Hebrew of the Hebrew scriptures. Its verb, for instance, makes provision for more than completed or continuing action for which the biblical Hebrew verb allows, but also for past and future times, subjunctive and indicative voices, and much else. The syntax is Indo-European in that we can translate the word order of the Mishnah into any Indo-European language and come up with perfect sense. None of that crabbed imitation of biblical Hebrew, that makes the Dead Sea scrolls an embarrassment to read, characterizes the Hebrew of the Mishnah. Mishnaic style is elegant, subtle, exquisite in its sensitivity to word order and repetition, balance, pattern.

The solution to the problem of the authority of the Mishnah, that is, its relationship to scripture, was worked out in the period after the closure of the Mishnah. Since no one now could credibly claim to sign the name of Ezra or Adam to a book of this kind, and since biblical Hebrew had provided no apologetic aesthetics whatever, the only options lay elsewhere. The two options were (1) to provide a myth of the origin of the contents of the Mishnah, and (2) to link each allegation of the Mishnah, through processes of biblical (not Mishnaic) exegesis, to verses of the scriptures. These two procedures together would establish for the Mishnah that standing that the uses to which the document was to be put demanded for it: a place in the canon of Israel and a legitimate relationship to the Torah of Moses. There were several ways in which the work went forward. These are represented by diverse documents that succeeded and dealt with the Mishnah. Let me now state the three principal possibilities. (1) The Mishnah required no systematic support through exegesis of scripture in light of Mishnaic laws. (2) The Mishnah by itself provided no reliable information, and all of its propositions demanded linkage to scripture, to which the Mishnah must be shown to be subordinate and secondary. (3) The Mishnah is an autonomous document but closely correlated with scripture.

The first extreme is represented by the Abot, ca. 250 C.E., which represents the authority of the sages cited in Abot as autonomous of scripture. Those authorities in Abot do not cite verses of scripture, but what they say does constitute a statement of the Torah. There can be no clearer way of saying that what these authorities present in and of itself falls into the classification of the Torah. The authorship of the Tosefta, ca. 400 C.E., takes the middle position. It very commonly cites a passage of the Mishnah and then adds to that passage an appropriate proof text. That is a quite common mode of supplementing the Mishnah. The mediating view if further taken by the Yerushalmi and the Bavli, ca. 400-600. With the Yerushalmi's authorship, that of the Bavli developed a well-crafted theory of the Mishnah and its relationship to scripture. Each rule of the Mishnah is commonly introduced in the exegesis supplied by the two Talmuds with the question, "What is the source of this statement?" And the answer invariably is, "As it is said" or " . . . written," with a verse of scripture, that is, the written Torah, then cited. The upshot is that the source of the rules of the Mishnah (and other writings) is scripture, not free-standing logic. The far extreme—everything in the Mishnah makes sense only as a (re)statement of scripture or upon scripture's authority—is taken by the Sifra, a post-Mishnaic compilation of exegeses on Leviticus, redacted at an indeterminate point, perhaps about 300 C.E. The Sifra systematically challenges reason (=the Mishnah) unaided by revelation (that is, exegesis of scripture) to sustain positions taken by the Mishnah, which is cited verbatim, and everywhere proves that it cannot be done.

The final and normative solution to the problem of the authority of the Mishnah worked out in the third and fourth centuries produced the myth of the dual Torah, oral and written, which formed the indicative and definitive trait of the Judaism that emerged from late antiquity. Tracing the unfolding of that myth leads us deep into the processes by which that Judaism took shape. The two Talmuds know the theory that there is a tradition separate from and in addition to the written Torah. This tradition it knows as "the teachings of scribes." There is ample evidence, implicit in what happens to the Mishnah in the Bavli, to allow a reliable description of how the Bavli's founders viewed the Mishnah. That view may be stated very simply. The Mishnah rarely cites verses of scripture in support of its propositions. The Bavli routinely adduces scriptural bases for the Mishnah's laws. The Mishnah seldom undertakes the exegesis of verses of scripture for any purpose. The Bavli consistently investigates the meaning of verses of scripture and does so for a variety of purposes. Accordingly, the Bavli, subordinate as it is to the Mishnah, regards the Mishnah as subordinate to and contingent upon scripture. That is why, in the Bavli's view, the Mishnah requires the support of proof texts of scripture. By itself, the Mishnah exercises no autonomous authority and enjoys no independent standing or norm-setting status.

The Talmud's Presentation of a System in the Form of Tradition

This brings us back, by a circuitous route, to the Bavli's authorship's explanation of its own position in relationship to the received "tradition," that is, to prior systemic statements, the Pentateuch's and the Mishnah's in particular. Their solution to the problem of the standing and authority of the Mishnah dictated their answer to the question of the representation, within a received tradition, of their own system as well. It was through phrase-by-phrase commentary that the Bavli's authorship justified the Mishnah as tradition and represented it as a secondary elaboration of scripture or as invariably resting on the authority of scripture. That form, as we realize, does what can be done to represent sentences of the Mishnah as related to sentences of scripture. That mode of writing, moreover, accomplished what we may call the dismantling or deconstruction of the system of the Mishnah and the reconstruction of its bits and pieces into the system of the Bavli. The Bavli's authorship never represented the Mishnah's system whole and complete, and it rarely acknowledged that the Mishnah consisted of more than discrete statements to be related to some larger cogent law that transcended the Mishnah.

Having represented the Mishnah as it did, the Bavli's authorship quite naturally chose to represent its own system in the same way, that is, as a mere elaboration of a received tradition, a stage in the sedimentary and incremental process by which the Torah continued to come down from Sinai. And for that purpose, the mixed logics embodied in the joining of philosophical and propositional statements on the principle of fixed association— commentary attached to a prior text—served exceedingly well. That explains how in the Bavli we have, in the (deceptive) form of a tradition, what is in fact an autonomous system connected with prior systems but not continuous with them. The authorship represented their own statement of an ethos, ethics, and defined social entity precisely as they did the received ones, the whole forming a single, seamless Torah revealed by God to Moses at Sinai. So much for a system to which the standing of tradition is imputed through formal means.

The Bible of Christianity

When we come to the counterpart religious world, we confront Christian intellectuals who are dealing also with the inheritance of ancient Israel's scriptures and facing the same problem. The parallel is exact in yet another aspect. Just as the authorship of the Bavli received not only what they came to call the written Torah but also the Mishnah and other writings that had attained acceptance, hence authority, from the closure of the Mishnah to their own day, so too did the Christian intellectuals inherit more than the Old Testament. They had in hand a variety of authoritative documents to which the inspiration of the Holy Spirit was imputed. So they confronted the same problem as faced the authorship of the Bavli, and it was in pretty much the same terms, namely, how to sort out received documents, each of which makes its own statement[5], takes up a different problem, and follows a different solution to that problem.

The Christian intellectuals joined together the received writings as autonomous books but imputed to the whole the standing of a single, coherent, and cogent statement—a harmonious Christian truth. This they did in the work of making the biblical canon,[6] joining diverse traditions into one, single, uniform, and therefore (putatively) harmonious Bible: God's word. Again, that explains my view that the Christian solution to the problem of making a statement but also situating that system in relationship to received tradition is to be characterized as imputing system to discrete traditions through a declared canon. Thus, as in the title of this chapter, the comparison of the solutions that would prevail respectively in Judaism's Bavli and Christianity's Bible are characterized as a system to which the standing of tradition is imputed—but against traditions, to which the form of a single system is, through the canonization of scriptures as the Bible, imputed.[7] The legitimacy of my comparing the two intellects

through their ultimate statements, the Bavli and the Bible, seems
to me sustained by the simple theological judgment of H.E.W.
Turner:

> The mind of the church [in making the canon] was guided by
> criteria rationally devised and flexibly applied. There is no
> dead hand in the production of the canon; there is rather the
> living action of the Holy Spirit using as he is wont the full range
> of the continuing life of the church to achieve his purposes in
> due season.[8]

I can find no better language to state, in a way interior to a system,
the claim that a writing or a set of writings constitutes a system:
a way of life, a world view, an address to a particular social entity.
This too is made explicit by Turner, who I take to be a thoroughly
reliable representative of Christian theology on the subject:

> There can be no doubt that the Bible is fundamentally an
> orthodox book, sufficient if its teaching is studied as a whole to
> lead to orthodox conclusions . . . The biblical data insist upon
> arranging themselves in certain theological patterns and cannot
> be forced into other moulds without violent distortion. That is
> the point of a famous simile of St. Irenaeus. The teaching of
> Scripture can be compared to a mosaic of the head of a king,
> but the heretics break up the pattern and reassemble it in the
> form of a dog or a fox.[9]

A master of the Bavli could not have said it better in claiming
both the systemic character, and the traditional standing, of his
statement.

Let me hasten to qualify the comparison at hand. In claiming
that a single problem of relating a system to tradition, for Judaism,
or traditions into a system, for Christianity, found two solutions
in the Bavli and the Bible respectively. I do not for one minute
suggest that the two groups of intellectuals were thinking along
the same lines at all. Quite to the contrary, the comparison
derives from a different standpoint altogether. When the Christian
theologians worked out the idea of "the Bible," consisting of "the
Old Testament and the New Testament," and when the Judaic
theologians worked out the idea of "the dual Torah," consisting
of "the written Torah and the oral Torah," did each group propose

to answer a question confronting the other group as well? We answer negative. For, as a matter of fact, each party pursued a problem particular to the internal logic and life of its own group. True, as a matter of necessity, each party had to designate within the larger corpus of scriptures deriving from ancient Israel those writings that it regarded as authoritative, therefore divinely revealed. But did the one side do so for the same reasons and within the same sort of theological logic that the other did? Each party had further to explain to itself and the end result, that is, the revealed words as a whole. What are they all together, all at once? The one party characterized the whole as a single Bible, a book, a piece of writing. The other party characterized the whole as a single Torah, revelation in two media: the one, writing; the other, memory. But these characterizations of the result of revelation, that is, of the canon, hardly constitute intersecting statements.

The reason that traditions became a system for Christianity, as Turner testifies was the intent of the outcome, derives from the life of the church, not from the issue of culture in its relationship to the logic of cogent discourse that I have framed here. Let us briefly review the formation of the received, traditional writings into a system, that is, as Turner says, a canon, a pattern of Christian truth. In the centuries after the Gospels were written, the church had to come to a decision whether, in addition to the scriptures of ancient Israel, there would be a further corpus of authoritative writing. The church affirmed that there would be, and the New Testament as counterpart to the Old Testament evolved into the canon. When we speak of canon we refer, in Childs's words, to "the process of theological interpretation by a faith community [that] left its mark on a literary text which did not continue to evolve and which became the normative interpretation of the events to which it bore witness for those identifying with that religious community."

Christians from the very beginning revered the Hebrew scriptures as "the Old Testament," regarding these writings as their sacred book. They denied the Jews any claim to the book, accusing them of misinterpreting it. The Old Testament served, in Harnack's words, to prove "that the appearance and the entire history of Jesus had been predicted hundreds and even thousands of years ago; and futher, that the founding of the New People which was to be fashioned out of all the nations upon earth had from the very beginning been prophesied and prepared for."[10] The text of the Hebrew scriptures supplied proofs for various propositions of theology, law, and liturgy. It served as a source of precedents: "if God had praised or punished this or that in the past, how much more . . . are we to look for similar treatment from him, we who are now living in the last days and who have received 'the calling of promise.'" Even after the rise of the New Testament, much of the Old Testament held its own. And, Harnack concludes, "The New Testament as a whole did not generally play the same role as the Old Testament in the mission and practice of the church."

In the beginning the church did not expect the canon—now meaning only the Hebrew scriptures—to grow through Christian additions. As Cross says, "In the new covenant the sole complement to the Word in the Torah was the Word made flesh in Christ." So it would be some time before a Christian canon, encompassing not only the received writings but the writings of the new age, would come into being. For until the time at hand, the Bible of the church consisted of the Hebrew scriptures, "the Old Testament." Before Marcion the Bible of the church was the Hebrew scriptures, pure and simple. While Filson assigns to the years between 160 and 175 the crystallization of the concept of the canon, the process came to the end by the end of the fourth century. Filson states, "There was no longer any wide dispute over the right of any of our twenty-seven books to a place in the New Testament canon." What was not a settled question for Eusebius in 330 had been worked out in the next span of time. So, in general, when we take up the issue of the canon of Christianity, we find ourselves in the third and fourth centuries.[11] The bulk of the work was complete by 200, with details under debate for another two hundred years.[12] The orthodoxy in which "the canon of an Old and a New Testament was firmly laid down" did not come into being overnight. From the time of Irenaeus the church affirmed the bipartite Christian Bible, containing the Old, and parallel with this and controlling it, the New Testament.[13] But what was to be in the New Testament, and when were the limits of the canon decided? Von Campenhausen concludes the description for us:

> [The Muratorian fragment] displays for the first time the concept of a collection of New Testament scriptures, which has deliberately been closed, and the individual books of which are regarded as "accepted" and ecclesiastically "sanctified," that is to say. . . . they have been "incorporated" into the valid corpus. We have thus arrived at the end of the long journey which leads to a New Testament thought of as "canonical" in the strict sense. Only one thing is still lacking: the precise name for this collection, which will make it possible to refer to the new Scripture as a unity and thus at one and the same time both to distinguish it from the old Scriptures and combine it with them in a new totality. . . . This is the last feature still wanting to the accomplishment of the bipartite Christian Bible.[14]

When does the Old Testament join the New as the Bible? Von Campenhausen makes a striking point. There was no need to look for a single name for the entire document. There was no such thing as an Old Testament or a New Testament as a single physical entity. To the eye, the whole canon was still fragmented into a series of separate rolls or volumes. Von Campenhausen makes a still more relevant point:

> There was no reason why in themselves the two parts of the Bible should not have different names. In the early period one possibility suggested itself almost automatically: if one had the New and the Old Testament in mind, one could speak of the "Gospel" and the "Law."[15]

The use of "Old" and "New" Testament represents a particular theology. It was from the beginning of the third century that scripture for orthodox Christianity consisted of an Old and a New Testament. So, we conclude, "Both the Old and the New Testaments had in essence already reached their final form and significance around the year 200."[16] For Christianity, the authority of the Bible rested on the reliability of the biblical record of the predictions of Christ in the prophets and the testimony to

Christ of the apostles.[17] The biblical component of the "canon of truth" proved contingent, not absolute and dominant.

We now realize that the issues important to the Judaism of the sages were in no way consubstantial with, let alone comparable to, the issues at hand. None of the cited theological precipitants for the canonical process in a Judaic formulation played any role I can discern in the theory of the Torah in two media. The myth of the dual Torah, which functioned as a canonical process, validating as it did the writings of sages as part of Torah from Sinai, derives from neither the analogy to the Old Testament process nor, to begin with, from the narrow issue of finding a place for the specific writings of rabbis within the larger Torah. And, it follows, *we cannot refer to "the Bible" when we speak of Judaism.*

When scholars of the formation of the canon of Christianity use the word canon, they mean: (1) the recognition of sacred scripture over and beyond the (received) Hebrew scriptures, (2) the identification of writings revered within the church as canonical, hence authoritative, (3) the recognition that these accepted writings formed a scripture which (4) served as the counterpart to the Hebrew scriptures; hence (5) the formation of the Bible as the Old and New Testaments. Now, as a matter of fact, none of these categories, stage by stage, corresponds in any way to the processes in the unfolding of the holy books of the sages, which I shall now describe in terms of Torah. But the word "Torah" in the context of the writings of the sages at hand in no way forms that counterpart to the word "canon" as used (quite correctly) by Childs, von Campenhausen, and others. Moreover the word "Bible" and the word "Torah" in no way speak of the same thing; I mean, they do not refer to the same category or classification.

Judaism's System as Tradition; Christianity's Traditions as System

The statement of the Bavli is, in fact, not a canonical system at all. For in the mode of presentation of the Bavli's system, revelation does not close or reach conclusion. God speaks all the time through the sages. Representing the whole as "Torah" means that the Bavli speaks a tradition formed in God's revelation of God's will to Moses, our rabbi. Ancient Israel's scriptures fall into the category of Torah, but they do not fill that category up. Other writings fall into that same category. By contrast, canon refers to particular books that enjoy a distinctive standing; Torah refers to various things that fall into a particular classification. The Christian canon reached closure with the Bible: Old and New Testaments. The Judaic Torah never closed: revelation of Torah continued.[18] The Torah is not the Bible, and the Bible is not the Torah. The Bible emerges from the larger process of establishing church order and doctrine.[19] The Torah, oral and written, for its part derives from the larger process of working out in relationship to the Pentateuchal system the authority and standing of two successive and connected systems that had followed: the Mishnah, then the Bavli.

A long-standing problem faced all system-builders in the tradition that commenced with the Pentateuch. From that original system onward, system builders, both in Judaism and, as we now realize, in Christianity, would have to represent their system not as an original statement on its own but as part of a tradition of revealed truth. Not only so, but in the passage of time and in the accumulation of writing, Christian and Judaic intellectuals would have to work out logics that would permit cogent discourse within the inherited traditions and with them. In the Christian case, the solution to the problem lay in accepting as canonical a variety of documents, each with its own logic. We note, for instance, that extraordinarily cogent communication could be accomplished in some Christian writings through symbol and not through proposition at all. Christian writings exhibit each its own coherent logical principles of cogency, with the making of connections and the drawing of conclusions fully consistent throughout.

The final solution of the canon sidestepped the problem of bringing these logics together within a single statement. If diverse logics work, each for its own authoritative writing, then I do not have to effect coherence among diverse logics at all. And the canon, the conception of the Bible, would impose from without a cogency of discourse difficult to discern in the interior of the canonical writings. That decision would then dictate the future of the Christian intellectual enterprise: to explore the underbrush of the received writing and to straighten out the tangled roots. No wonder, then, that in philosophy, culminating in the return to Athens, the Christian mind would recover that glory of logical and systematic order denied it in the dictated canon, the Bible. But the canon did solve the problem that faced the heirs to a rather odd corpus of writing. Ignoring logic as of no account, accepting considerable diversity in modes of making connections and drawing conclusions, the traditional solution represented a better answer than the librarians of the Essenes at Qumran had found, which was to set forth (so far as matters now seem, at any rate) neither a system nor a canon.

The Bavli's authorship was the first in the history of Judaism (encompassing Christianity in its earliest phases[20]) to take up, in behalf of its distinct and distinctive system, a position of relationship with the received heritage of tradition, with a corpus of truth assigned to God's revelation to Moses at Sinai. The framers of the Pentateuch did not do so; rather, they said that what they wrote was the work of God, having been dictated to Moses at Sinai. The Essene librarians at Qumran did not do so. They collected this and that, never even pretending that everything fit together in some one way, not as commentary to scripture (though some wrote commentaries), not as systemic statements (though the library included such statements), and not as a canon (unless everything we find in the detritus forms a canon by definition). The authorship of the Mishnah did not do so. Quite to the contrary, that authorship undertook the pretense that, even when scripture supplied facts and even dictated the order of the facts, their writing was new and fresh and their own.[21] No wonder that the Mishnah's authorship resorted to its own logic to make its own statement in its own language and for its own purposes. No wonder, too, that the hubris of the Mishnah's authorship provoked the systematic demonstration of the dependence of the Mishnah on scripture; also the allegation that the Mishnah stood as an autonomous statement, another Torah — the oral one — coequal with the written Torah. The hubris of the great intellects of Judaic and Christian antiquity, the daring authorships of the Pentateuch and the Mishnah, the great ecclesiastical minds behind the Bible, reached boldest realization in the Bavli. This authorship accomplished, through its ingenious joining of two distinct and contradictory logics of cogent discourse, the statement of the Torah in its own rhetoric, following its own logic, and in accord with its own designated topical program. But hubris is not the sole trait that characterizes the Jewish mind, encompassing its Christian successors, in classical times.

There is a second trait common to them all. It is that in all systemic constructions and statements the issues of logic responded to the systemic imperative and in no way dictated the shape and structure of that imperative. The system invariably proves to be prior, recapitulating itself also in its logic. And however diverse the issues addressed by various systems made up by the Jewish mind in classical times, all had to address a single question natural to the religious ecology in which Judaic systems flourished. That question, in the aftermath of the Pentateuchal system, concerned how people could put together in a fresh construction and a composition of distinctive proportions a statement that purported to speak truth to a social entity that, in the nature of things, already had truth. This framing of the issue of how system contradicts tradition, how the logic that tells me to make a connection of this to that but not to the other thing, and to draw from that connection one conclusion rather than some other — that framing of the issue places intellect and the formation of mind and modes of thought squarely into the ongoing processes dictated by the givens of society.

Why, then, characterize the Bavli's system builders as the climax of the hubris of the Jewish intellectuals? Because the Bavli's authorship was the first in the history of Judaism, encompassing Christianity in its earliest phases, to take up in behalf of its distinct and distinctive system a position of relationship with the received heritage of tradition, with a corpus of truth assigned to God's revelation to Moses at Sinai. Prior systems had stood on their own, beginning with that of the Pentateuch itself in ca. 450 B.C.E. Four centuries after the Mishnah — in their minds, eighteen centuries after God revealed the Torah to Moses at Sinai — the Bavli's authorship remade the two received systems, the Pentateuchal and the Mishnaic. In its own rhetoric, in accord with its own topical program, appealing to a logic unique to itself among all Jewish minds in ancient times, that authorship presented the Torah of Sinai precisely as it wished to represent it. And it did so defiantly, not discretely and by indirection: not merely alleging that Moses had written it all down, like the Pentateuchal compilers; or modestly identifying with the direction of the Holy Spirit the choices that it made, like the Christians responsible for making the Bible; or even, as with the framers of the Mishnah, sedulously sidestepping, in laconic and disingenuous innocence, the issue of authority and tradition entirely. Quite the opposite, the Bavli's intellectuals took over the entire tradition, scriptural and Mishnaic alike, chose what they wanted, tacked on to the selected passages their own words in their own way, and then put it all out as a single statement of their own.

True, they claimed for their system the standing of mere amplification of that tradition. As a matter of fact, however, they did say it all in their own words, and they did set forth the whole of their statement in their own way. Without recapitulating the received choices of ignoring or merely absorbing the received revelation, they represented as the one whole Torah revealed by God to Moses, our rabbi, at Sinai what they themselves had made up, and they made it stick. And that, I think, is the supreme hubris of the Jewish mind from the beginnings, in the Pentateuch to the conclusion and climax in the Bavli. I like to think that that hubris of theirs, at least for the beauty of it, explains the success of what they made up—on the simple principle: the more daring, the more plausible.

A concluding prayer:

God,
now that we like each other, help us to understand as well that we do not
understand each
other—but can learn to.
God,
help us learn.
Speedily and soon.
Amen.

Notes

Preface

1 New York: Harper & Row, 1969.
2 Chicago: University of Chicago Press, 1987.

3. The Fourth-Century Confrontation of Christianity and Judaism:
I. History and Messiah

1 Cited by Robert L. Wilken, *The Christians As the Romans Saw Them* (New Haven: Yale University Press, 1984), 32-33.

2 *Church History* 10:1, 6-7, trans, Arthur Cushman McGiffert, in *Nicene and Post-Nicene Fathers of the Christian Church*, 2d series, ed. Philip Schaff and Henry Wace (reprint Grand Rapids: Wm B. Eerdmans, 1961), 1:369.

3 Eusebius, *Ecclesiastical History*, Bk. X, ch. 1.

4 All quoted passages from Colm Luibheid, *Eusebius of Caesarea and the Arian Crisis* (Ireland: Irish Academic Press, 1981), 13–15.

5 Hans Lietzmann, *A History of the Early Church*, vol. 3, trans. B.L. Woolf (London: Lutterworth Press and Cleveland: World Publishing Co., 1950), 166, 169.

6 I draw on my *Messiah in Context: Israel's History and Destiny in Formative Judaism* (Philadelphia: Fortress Press, 1984).

7 I think we would go too far were we to impute to Eusebius the notion that, just as the resurrection put all of history into a new light, so the advent of the Christian emperor likewise required the rereading of the entire past. But the point of contact in the otherwise extravagant comparison is simple. Both events were one-time, unique, and for that reason, enormously important.

8 As I said, we do not know that it was in response to the crisis of Constantine's Christian empire that sages composed Genesis Rabbah—their vast expansion of the Book of Genesis to encompass their own time. We only know what they said and the context in which they said it.

9 Rosemary Radford Ruether, *Faith and Fratricide: The Theological Roots of Anti-Semitism* (New York: Seabury Press, 1974), 173.

10 Wilkin, *The Christians*, pp. 32-3, 66-7, 76, 132, xvi. On "anti-Semitism," compare John G. Gager, *The Origins of Anti-Semitism: Attitudes Toward Judaism in Pagan and Christian Antiquity* (New York: Oxford University Press, 1983): "The very violence of Chrysostom's language demonstrates the potential for a linkage between anti-Jewish beliefs and anti-Semitic feelings."

11 Wilken, *The Christians*, 155-8.

12 Ibid., 160.

13 Ibid., 158.

14 Ibid., 149.

15 The Talmud of the Land of Israel totally ignores whatever messianic hopes and figures took part in the fiasco of Julian's projected rebuilding of the Temple.

4. The Fourth-century Confrontation of Christianity and Judaism:
II.   *Who is Israel? The Aftermath*

1 Ruether, *Faith and Fratricide*, 64ff.

2 Ibid., pp. 64ff., see also Gager, *The Origins of Anti-Semitism*, 256-8.

3 Adolf Harnack, *The Mission and Expansion of Christianity in the First Three Centuries* (New York: Harper & Bros., 1962), 241, 244.

4 *The Proof of the Gospel I 2:*, cited by Luibheid, *Eusebius*, 41.

5 Harnack, *Mission and Expansion*, 256-57.

6 See my *Aphrahat*, 150-195.

7 It suffices to note, following Rosemary Ruether's letter (June 25, 1986), the following: "This protection of the Jews and Judaism, even if under hostile and punitive laws, flowed from one aspect of that same Christian theology that saw itself as God's elect *vis à vis* a superceded Judaism. Just as the Jews saw Christian Rome as a "brother" but a discarded brother, so Christianity saw Judaism as brother, but as unbelieving brother. To reconcile the conflict it constructed an eschatology that mandated eventual Jewish conversion and reconciliation to Christianity (on Christian terms, of course). This notion that the Jews had a future destiny in God's design for history required the survival of the Jews as a religious community. In Christian eschatology the Jews as a religious group had finally to accept Jesus as the Christ and be included in redemption. In this backhanded way Christianity acknowledged that the Jews were still God's chosen people and could not be simply discarded by God."

8 David Berger, *The Jewish-Christian Debate in the High Middle Ages* (Philadelphia, Jewish Publication Society of America 1979), 13 Cf. p. 11: "Christians were genuinely puzzled at the Jewish failure to accept the overwhelming array of scriptural arguments which they had marshalled."

9 Twelfth century: ibid., 7, n. 2: Anti-Christian works by Jews . . . are virtually nonexistent before the twelfth century. Berger's judgment: 8.

10 Hyam Maccoby, *Judaism on Trial: Jewish-Christian Disputations in the Middle Ages* (Rutherford, N. J.: Farleigh Dickinson University Press, 1981) 11, 23, 26-38, 41-42.

11 Ibid., 82-96.

12 Ibid., 86, 89.

5. The Absoluteness of Christianity and the Uniqueness of Judaism

1 I refer to the appendix, "Orality, Hermenutics, and the Judaism beyond the Texts," in my *Oral Tradition in Judaism: The Case of the Mishnah*, The Albert Bates Lord Studies in Oral Tradition, Vol. 1 (New York: Tarland Publishing, Inc.), 149-60.

2 Joseph A. Schumpeter, *History of Economic Analysis* (New York: Oxford University Press, 1954), 54.

3 *A History of the Mishnaic Law of Purities*, III, "Kelim" (Leiden: E.J. Brill, 1974), 374ff.

4 The ecumenical movement that encompasses Christianity and Islam and Christianity and Buddhism does not insist upon the same intersections, e.g., that Christianity can be understood only in the context of Muhammed's life and teachings or Buddha's. So there can be such interreligious dialogue as is possible without those foundations that scholarship, distinct from theology, is supposed to be able to lay down. But I do not see a future for religious dialogue between Christianity and Judaism until each party understands that it cannot understand what is unique to the other, which is to say, what makes the other other.

5 See the excellent discussion by E.P. Sanders on "Jesus and the Temple" in his *Jesus and Judaism* (London: SCM Press and Philadelphia: Fortress Press, 1985), 61-76.

6 Ibid., 64.

7 Ibid., 70.

8 Ibid., 75.

9 This seems to me not yet fully appreciated in the available literature, ably summarized by Sanders.

10 I have presented the entire textual representation in my *History of the Mishnaic Law of Appointed Times*, III, "Sheqalim, Yoma, Sukkah. Translation and Explanation" (Leiden: E.J. Brill, 1982), 8-15.

11 Can we impute wide circulation in the first century to the contents of a statement of the Tosefta in amplification of the Mishnah, an authorship of ca. 300 C.E. addressing a document of ca. 300 C.E.? In this instance, there is a simple reason for thinking so. Since Exod. 30:16 is explicit in the matter, I am not inclined to doubt that the interpretation of the atoning power and expiatory effect of the daily whole offering circulated in the first century. On the contrary, if scripture is explicit, then people will have known the meaning of the rite; it was a commonplace. And for the same reason, I see no grounds for doubting that people generally grasped the reason for the presence of the money-changers, who as is clear, simply facilitated an essential rite of all Israel.

12 In fact, we deal with diverse groups talking to diverse audiences, a set of Judaic and Christian religious systems, respectively. How they form two distinct sets is not the problem of this study.

13 Judaic interest in Christianity has never proved more motivated by curiosity and good will than Christian interest in Judaism. For nearly a thousand years, Judaic writing on Christianity was trivial and merely scurrilous. The advent of the disputations of the Middle Ages changed that, but conditions hardly served to encourage a considered exchange of reasoned views, to state matters mildly. So in no way do Christians bear the entire onus for the incapacity of Judaism and Christianity to engage with one another.

14 Along these same lines, Judaism no longer pretends Christianity is simply not there, or if there, has never made a difference to Judaism and makes no difference now. That isolationist and triumphalist position no longer predominates, though it is paramount in orthodox Judaic response to the Judeo-Christian encounter.

6. Shalom:
Complementarity

1 Address at the Uomini e religioni conference, Warsaw, Poland, August 31, 1989, commemorating the 50th anniversary of the beginning of World War II.
2 Philip C. Almond, *The British Discovery of Buddhism* (Cambridge: Cambridge University Press, 1989), 4.
3 Ibid., 139-40.
4 Ibid., 140.

8. Judaism and Christianity:
The Bavli and the Bible

1 It is not pertinent to deal with *tradition* as a correlative source of God's truth, and I take no position on controverted issues of theology of Christianity as to whether solely scripture, or also scripture and tradition preserved by the teaching authority of the church, constitute the authoritative repository of revelation.
2 Much that is said here can be said also of the Yerushalmi. But I should claim that the authorships of Leviticus Rabbah, Genesis Rabbah, Pesiqta deRab Kahana, and other compilations of thought set forth in close relationship to the written Torah had also to think through the same problem of the relationship of received truth to the autonomous thought of a well-composed system. What I say of the Bavli's authorship's intellect pertains to the other authorships within the canon of the Judaism of the dual Torah as it reached conclusion in late antiquity. But I readily admit that each authorship has to be read in its own documentary setting, and only at the end of that considerable process can the generalizations offered here, resting on what I see as the Bavli's authorship's solution to the shared problem of sorting out the interplay of system and tradition, be refined and correctly restated to cover the whole of the canon.
3 This is, of course, a Roman Catholic reading of the formation of the Bible, treating the Bible as the creation and gift of the church, rather than according to its autonomous theological standing as the principal medium for the statement of the orthodoxy. But it seems to me that the history of the creation of the Bible requires that reading.
4 I have spelled these matters out for the second through the sixth divisions of the Mishnah in my *History of the Mishnaic Law* (Leiden: E.J. Brill, 1974-1985) in forty-three volumes. For each tractate I show how the topic at hand was analyzed by the tractate's framers, proving that what they identified as the problematic of the topic instructed those writers on what they wanted to know about the topic and also on the correct, logical order in which they would state the results of their inquiry.
5 Whether that is a systemic statement or not, and for the present purpose, the analysis of systemic compositions and constructions within the Christian framework is not required. My purpose is solely to place into relationship two solutions to the problem of system and tradition. While an analysis of the systemic traits of Christian writings down to the canonization of the (Christian) Bible (the Old Testament and the New Testament) in my judgment would prove exceedingly suggestive, it has not been done, and I cannot pretend to be able to do it. As is clear, I conceive the Bible to represent a solution to a problem of the same order as that solved, through

the formal including the logical traits of the Bavli, by the Bavli's authorship. But beyond that point, I cannot go, e.g., I cannot judge whether or not we find Christian systems only in Irenaeus, Origen, and Augustine, as seems to me the case, or also in other writings, circles, documents, and the like; whether or not theology, in Christianity, forms a counterpart to the system building that yielded the Mishnah, the Yerushalmi, the Bavli, and other writings in the Judaism of the dual Torah, and so on and so forth.

6 I hasten to add, they did so not only in the process of the canonization of some writings as the Old Testament and the New Testament, the Bible. It seems to me the work of framing creeds, preparing liturgies to be used throughout the church(es), debating theology, and the like all attended to the same labor of stating the pattern of Christian truth out of the received writings, all of them claiming to derive from the Holy Spirit or to be consonant with writings that did, that competed for standing and that contradicted one another on pretty much every important point. Once more, I underline that in dealing only with the work of canon, I in no way pretend to address the broader issues implicit in the topic as I have defined it.

7 In laying matters out, I avoid entering the issues debated by Walter Bauer, *Orthodoxy and Heresy in Earliest Christianity* (Philadelphia: Fortress Press and London: SCM Press 1971), and H.E.W. Turner, *The Pattern of Christian Truth. A Study of the Relations between Orthodoxy and Heresy in the Early church 1954* (London: A.R. Mowbray & Co. Ltd., 1954). I do claim that my representation of matters accords with Turner's chapter, "Orthodoxy and the Bible," 241ff.

8 Turner, *The Pattern*, 258.

9 Ibid., 300.

10 Brevard S. Childs, *The New Testament as Canon* (London: SCM Press and Philadelphia: Fortress Press 1985) 26; Adolf Harnack, *The Mission and Expansion of Christianity in the First Three Centuries* (New York: Harper & Bros., 1962) 283-4.

11 Hans Von Campenhausen, *The Formation of the Christian Bible* (Philadelphia: Fortress Press, 1972), 147.

12 Childs, *Canon*, 18.

13 Von Campenhausen, *Formation*, 209.

14 Ibid., 261-62.

15 Ibid.

16 Ibid., 327.

17 Ibid., 330.

18 So, too, did the pattern of Christian truth, but in a different form and forum from the canonical Bible.

19 I cannot pretend to know whether or not von Campenhausen's arguments about the emergence of the New Testament in response to Montanism prove valid. I can flatly state that the issue—providing a basis to sort out the claims of living prophets, with direct access to divine teachings—bears no point of intersection, let alone comparison and contrast with anything known to me in the entire corpus of rabbinic writing of late antiquity.

20 I do not mean to ignore the school of Matthew and the numerous other Christian writers who cited proof texts for their propositions. But as in the case of their Judaic counterparts, merely citing proof texts is not the same thing as setting forth a complete *system* in the form of a *tradition*, such as was done by the Bavli's authorship.

21 The best example is Mishnah-tractate Yoma, chaps. 1 through 7, which sedulously follow the order of Lev. 16 and review its rite step by step, rarely citing the pertinent chapter of scripture and never conceding that all that was in hand was a summary and paraphrase of rules available elsewhere. It is the simple fact that we cannot make any sense out of that tractate without a point-by-point consultation with Lev. 16. But there are numerous other examples of a mere paraphrase, by Mishnah's authorship, of passages of scripture (along with many more in which scripture has nothing to say on topics dealt with in the Mishnah, or in which what scripture thinks important about a topic is simply ignored as of no interest in the Mishnah).

General Index

Abin, salvation and Israel, 77
Age of Constantine: issues confronting
  Judaism and Christianity, 31–33
Almond, Philip C., 112–14
Ambrose, Saint, 32
Anti-Semitism and Roman Catholic
  church, 16, 27
Aphrahat: *Demonstration Sixteen*, 72;
  salvation and identification of
  Israel, 70–76, 79, 82, 91; shaping of
  history, 31, 36

Bar Kokhba, 38–39, 54, 56, 59–60
Berger, Peter, 89
Bible and Talmud: *See* Talmud and
  Bible
Bickerman, 32
Billerbeck, P., 93
Bun, messianism, 58

Childs, Brevard S., 146
Christianity: as "a" spiritual Judaism,
  16–29; *See also* Judaism and
  Christianity, Chrysostom, John,
  shaping of history, 31–32, 48–53,
  55–56, 63–64, 91
Common traits: each as family, 4;
  sanctification and salvation, 3–8,
  12–13
Constantine, 17, 30–37, 42, 47, 86, 92:
  See also Age of Constantine
Constantius, 85
Cross, F. L., 144

Diocletian, 32

Eleazar of Modiin, messianism, 60–61
Essenes, writings aiding new
  classicism of theologies of Judaism
  and Christianity, 25
Eusebius, 17; shaping of history, 31,
  34–41, 43, 47, 91

Evangelism: Judaism and Christianity
  in first century, 16–29; Paul's
  relation with Judaism, 16–17, 19,
  22, 26

Filson, F., 144

Gager, J., 68
Geffcken, 85–86
Gospel writers and range of enemies
  chosen by, 2
Gratian, 85
Greeley, Andrew and Jacob Neusner,
  *Our Bible: A Priest and a Rabbi Read
  the Scripture Together*, 123

Hanina, Rome in history of Israel, 46
Harnack, Adolf, 68, 70, 144
History: factors in its development,
  10–13; meaning of, 33–46; shaping
  of by sages, 30–64; theological errors
  concerning, 21–27;
Hunia, salvation and Israel, 78

Iamblichus, 85
Israel: Christianity as counterpart,
  79–92; its identity and messianism,
  30–84

Judah b. R. Simon, Rome and Israel,
  82
Judaism, surviving fourth century
  civilization, 84–92
Judaism and Christianity: beliefs,
  questions regarding, 1; Christianity
  as counterpart of Israel, 79–92;
  comparisons and differences, 1–2;
  Orthodoxy in first century, 21–22
Julian, 32–33, 53, 85
Justin, 103

Index of Biblical and Talmudic References